Survival Communications
in South Dakota

John E. Parnell, KK4HWX

13 – ISBN 978-1478172536
10 – ISBN 1478172533

Cover design by:
Lynda Colón
FREELANCE GRAPHIC DESIGN &
MARKETING COMMUNICATIONS
www.hirelynda.webs.com

Titles available in this series:

Survival Communications in Alabama
Survival Communications in Alaska
Survival Communications in Arizona
Survival Communications in Arkansas
Survival Communications in California
Survival Communications in Colorado
Survival Communications in Connecticut
Survival Communications in Delaware
Survival Communications in Florida
Survival Communications in Georgia
Survival Communications in Hawaii
Survival Communications in Idaho
Survival Communications in Illinois
Survival Communications in Indiana
Survival Communications in Iowa
Survival Communications in Kansas
Survival Communications in Kentucky
Survival Communications in Louisiana
Survival Communications in Maine
Survival Communications in Maryland
Survival Communications in Massachusetts
Survival Communications in Michigan
Survival Communications in Minnesota
Survival Communications in Mississippi
Survival Communications in Missouri

Survival Communications in Montana
Survival Communications in Nebraska
Survival Communications in Nevada
Survival Communications in New Hampshire
Survival Communications in New Jersey
Survival Communications in New Mexico
Survival Communications in New York
Survival Communications in North Carolina
Survival Communications in North Dakota
Survival Communications in Ohio
Survival Communications in Oklahoma
Survival Communications in Oregon
Survival Communications in Pennsylvania
Survival Communications in Rhode Island
Survival Communications in South Carolina
Survival Communications in South Dakota
Survival Communications in Tennessee
Survival Communications in Texas
Survival Communications in Utah
Survival Communications in Vermont
Survival Communications in Virginia
Survival Communications in Washington
Survival Communications in West Virginia
Survival Communications in Wisconsin
Survival Communications in Wyoming

The above titles are available from your favorite online or brick-and-mortar bookstore or directly from the publisher at Tutor Turtle Press LLC, 1027 S. Pendleton St. – Suite B-10, Easley, SC 29642 or on our website: www.TutorTurtlePress.com.

TABLE OF CONTENTS

Appendix A – South Dakota Ham Radio Clubs

ARRL Affiliated Radio Clubs in South Dakota – By City

Appendix B – FCC Amateur Radio Licenses in South Dakota by City

Survival Communications in South Dakota

Perhaps you have prepared for WTSHTF or TEOTWAWKI with respect to food, water, self-defense and shelter. But what about communication?

Whenever there is a disaster (hurricane, earthquake, economic collapse, nuclear war, EMF, solar eruption, etc.), the normal means of communication that we're all reliant upon (cell phone, land line phone, the Internet, etc.) will probably be, at best, sporadic and at worst, non-existent.

As this author sees it, short of smoke signals and mirrors, there are three options for communication in "trying times": (1) GMRS or FRS radios; (2) CB radios; and (3) ham or amateur radio. Let's consider each of these options to come up with the most acceptable one.

GMRS (General Mobile Radio Service) / FRS (Family Radio Service)

GMRS (General Mobile Radio Service) / FRS (Family Radio Service) radios work optimally over short distances where there is minimal interference. Originally designed to be used as pagers, particularly inside a building or other such confined area, these radios are low-cost and convenient to carry. Unfortunately their small size and light weight comes with a trade-off – short range and short battery life. These radios are supposed to be able to communicate for up to 25-30 miles. Right. That's on level terrain, without buildings or trees getting in the way. While battery life technology is constantly improving, you will need spare batteries to keep communicating or someway of recharging the ones in the radio. In this author's opinion, GMRS/FRS radios are not first choice when concerned with medium or long range communication.

CB (Citizens Band)

CB (Citizens Band) radios operate in a frequency range originally reserved for ham or amateur radio operation. Because of the overwhelming number of people wishing quick, low-cost, regulation-free communication, the FCC (Federal Communication Commission) split off a portion of the frequency spectrum and allowed anyone to purchase a CB radio and start communicating. No test. No license. Just personal/business communication. Today, CB radios are readily available in such outlets as eBay and Craigslist. This author has seen them at yard/garage/tag sales and at flea markets.

CB radios come in a variety of "flavors." Fixed units, sometimes referred to as base units are intended for home use. For the most part, they derive their power from the utility company. In the event of loss of electricity, most base units can also be connected to a 12-volt battery, like that in your car/truck. If you choose to obtain a fixed unit, make sure you know how to connect the unit to the battery – ahead of time. Trying to figure this out when you're under extra stress is not a good situation.

A second type of CB radio is designed to be mobile, that is, installed in your car/truck. It gets its power from the vehicle's battery. You can either attach an antenna permanently to the vehicle or have a removable, magnetic type antenna.

The third type of CB radio is designed for handheld use. They are small and light. Most weigh less than a pound and operate on batteries. Yes, using batteries in a CB poses the same limitations as those by the GMRS/FRS radios, but have the added advantage that most handheld units come with a cigarette lighter adapter. Comes in handy when you are on the move and wish to be able to communicate both from a vehicle and also when you have to abandon it.

While they have a greater range than GMRS/FRS radios, CB radios are, legally, limited to operate on 40 channels, with a power rating of four (4) watts or less. Yes, it is possible to alter CB radios to get around these limitations, but not legally,

Ham/Amateur Radio

Ham/Amateur radio is very appealing. With a ham radio, you are not limited to less than 50 miles, but can communicate with anyone in the world (who also has access to a ham radio, of course).

Standardized Amateur Radio Prepper Communications Plan

In the event of a nationwide catastrophic disaster, the nationwide network of Amateur Radio licensed preppers will need a set of standardized meeting frequencies to share information and coordinate activities between various prepper groups. This Standardized Amateur Radio Communications Plan establishes a set of frequencies on the 80 meter, 40 meter, 20 meter, and 2 meter Amateur Radio bands for use during these types of catastrophic disasters.

Routine nets will not be held on all of these frequencies, but preppers are encouraged to use them when coordinating with other preppers on a routine basis. Routine nets may be conducted by The American Preparedness Radio Net (TAPRN) on these or other frequencies as they see fit. However, TAPRN will promote the use of these standardized frequencies by all Amateur Radio licensed preppers during times of catastrophic disaster. The promotion of this Standardized Amateur Radio Communications Plan is encouraged by all means within the prepper community, including via Amateur Radio, Twitter, Facebook, and various blogs.

Standardized Frequencies and Modes

80 Meters – 3.818 MHz LSB (TAPRN Net: Sundays at 9 PM ET)
40 Meters – 7.242 MHz LSB
40 Meters Morse Code / Digital – 7.073 MHz USB (TAPRN: Sundays at 7:30 PM ET on CONTESTIA 4/250)
20 Meters – 14.242 MHz USB
2 Meters – 146.420 MHz FM

Nets and Network Etiquette

In times of nationwide catastrophic disaster, the ability of any one prepper to initiate and sustain themselves as a net control may be limited by the availability of power and other resource shortages. However, all licensed preppers are encouraged to maintain a listening watch on these frequencies as often as possible during a catastrophic disaster. Preppers may routinely announce themselves in the following manner:

• This is [Your Callsign Phonetically] in [Your State], maintaining a listening watch on [Standard Frequency] for any preppers on frequency seeking information or looking to provide information. Please call [Your Callsign Phonetically]. Preppers exchanging information that may require follow up should agree upon a designated time to return to the frequency and provide further information. If other stations are utilizing the frequency at the designated time you return, maintain watch and proceed with your communications when those stations are finished. If your communications are urgent and the stations on frequency are not passing information of a critical nature, interrupt with the word "Break" and request use of the frequency.

For More Information

Catastrophe Network: http://www.catastrophenetwork.org or @CatastropheNet on Twitter The American Preparedness Radio Network: http://www.taprn.com or @TAPRN on Twitter

© 2011 Catastrophe Network, Please Distribute Freely

In order to use a ham radio, legally, one must be licensed to do so by the FCC (other countries have analogous governmental bodies to regulate ham radio). To obtain a license is quite easy – take a test and pay your license fee. There are currently three classes of license – Technician, General, and Amateur Extra. With each of these licenses come specific abilities.

Technician class is the beginning level. The exam consists of 35 multiple choice questions randomly drawn from a pool of 395 questions. The question pool is readily available online for free downloading (http://www.ncvec.org/downloads/Revised%20Element%202.Pdf) or in such publications at *Ham Radio License Manual Revised 2nd Edition* (ISBN 978-0-87259-097-7). The current Technician pool of questions is to be used from July 1, 2010 to June 30, 2014. Be sure the question pool you are studying from is current. You will need to score at least 26 correct to pass. (Do not worry, Morse Code is no longer on the test, although many ham operators use it anyway.) You do not need to take a formal class in order to qualify to take the exam. You can learn the material on your own. Most people spend 10-15 hours studying and then successfully take the exam. The cost of taking the exam is under $20. The exam is given in MANY locations throughout the US. Usually the exam is given by area ham clubs. You do not have to belong to the club to take the exam. Check Appendix A for a listing of clubs in South Dakota.

Topics for the Technician License in Amateur Radio

The Technician license exam covers such topics as basic regulations, operating practices, and electronic theory, with a focus on VHF and UHF applications. Below is the syllabus for the Technician Class.

Subelement T1 – FCC Rules, descriptions and definitions for the amateur radio service, operator and station license responsibilities

[6 Exam Questions – 6 Groups]

T1A – Amateur Radio services; purpose of the amateur service, amateur-satellite service, operator/primary station license grant, where FCC rules are codified, basis and purpose of FCC rules, meanings of basic terms used in FCC rules

T1B – Authorized frequencies; frequency allocations, ITU regions, emission type, restricted sub-bands, spectrum sharing, transmissions near band edges

T1C – Operator classes and station call signs; operator classes, sequential, special event, and vanity call sign systems, international communications, reciprocal operation, station license licensee, places where the amateur service is regulated by the FCC, name and address on ULS, license term, renewal, grace period

T1D – Authorized and prohibited transmissions

T1E – Control operator and control types; control operator required, eligibility, designation of control operator, privileges and duties, control point, local, automatic and remote control, location of control operator

T1F – Station identification and operation standards; special operations for repeaters and auxiliary stations, third party communications, club stations, station security, FCC inspection

---

Subelement T2 – Operating Procedures

[3 Exam Questions – 3 Groups]

T2A – Station operation; choosing an operating frequency, calling another station, test transmissions, use of minimum power, frequency use, band plans

T2B – VHF/UHF operating practices; SSB phone, FM repeater, simplex, frequency offsets, splits and shifts, CTCSS, DTMF, tone squelch, carrier squelch, phonetics

T2C – Public service; emergency and non-emergency operations, message traffic handling

---

Subelement T3 – Radio wave characteristics, radio and electromagnetic properties, propagation modes

[3 Exam Questions – 3 Groups]

T3A – Radio wave characteristics; how a radio signal travels; distinctions of HF, VHF and UHF; fading, multipath; wavelength vs. penetration; antenna orientation

T3B – Radio and electromagnetic wave properties; the electromagnetic spectrum, wavelength vs. frequency, velocity of electromagnetic waves

T3C – Propagation modes; line of sight, sporadic E, meteor, aurora scatter, tropospheric ducting, F layer skip, radio horizon

Subelement T4 - Amateur radio practices and station setup

[2 Exam Questions – 2 Groups]

T4A – Station setup; microphone, speaker, headphones, filters, power source, connecting a computer, RF grounding

T4B – Operating controls; tuning, use of filters, squelch, AGC, repeater offset, memory channels

Subelement T5 – Electrical principles, math for electronics, electronic principles, Ohm's Law

[4 Exam Questions – 4 Groups]

T5A – Electrical principles; current and voltage, conductors and insulators, alternating and direct current

T5B – Math for electronics; decibels, electronic units and the metric system

T5C – Electronic principles; capacitance, inductance, current flow in circuits, alternating current, definition of RF, power calculations

T5D – Ohm's Law

Subelement T6 – Electrical components, semiconductors, circuit diagrams, component functions

[4 Exam Groups – 4 Questions]

T6A – Electrical components; fixed and variable resistors, capacitors, and inductors; fuses, switches, batteries

T6B – Semiconductors; basic principles of diodes and transistors

T6C – Circuit diagrams; schematic symbols

T6D – Component functions

Subelement T7 – Station equipment, common transmitter and receiver problems, antenna measurements and troubleshooting, basic repair and testing

[4 Exam Questions – 4 Groups]

T7A – Station radios; receivers, transmitters, transceivers

T7B – Common transmitter and receiver problems; symptoms of overload and overdrive, distortion, interference, over and under modulation, RF feedback, off frequency signals; fading and noise; problems with digital communications interfaces

T7C – Antenna measurements and troubleshooting; measuring SWR, dummy loads, feedline failure modes

T7D – Basic repair and testing; soldering, use of a voltmeter, ammeter, and ohmmeter

Subelement T8 – Modulation modes, amateur satellite operation, operating activities, non-voice communications

[4 Exam Questions – 4 Groups]

T8A – Modulation modes; bandwidth of various signals

T8B – Amateur satellite operation; Doppler shift, basic orbits, operating protocols

T8C – Operating activities; radio direction finding, radio control, contests, special event stations, basic linking over Internet

T8D – Non-voice communications; image data, digital modes, CW, packet, PSK31

Subelement T9 – Antennas, feedlines

[2 Exam Groups – 2 Questions]

T9A – Antennas; vertical and horizontal, concept of gain, common portable and mobile antennas, relationships between antenna length and frequency

T9B – Feedlines; types, losses vs. frequency, SWR concepts, matching, weather protection, connectors

Subelement T0 – AC power circuits, antenna installation, RF hazards

[3 Exam Questions – 3 Groups]

T0A – AC power circuits; hazardous voltages, fuses and circuit breakers, grounding, lightning protection, battery safety, electrical code compliance

T0B – Antenna installation; tower safety, overhead power lines

T0C – RF hazards; radiation exposure, proximity to antennas, recognized safe power levels, exposure to others

Once your name and call sign are available in the FCC database, you have the privilege of operating on all VHF (2 m) and UHF (70 cm) frequencies above 30 megahertz (MHz) and HF frequencies 80, 40, and 15 meter, and on the 10 meter band using Morse code (CW), voice, and digital mode. For a Technician license in South Dakota, your call sign will consist of a two-letter prefix beginning with K or W, the number zero (0), and a three-letter suffix. The single digit number in the call sign is determined according to which area of the US you obtain your first license. Even though you may move to another state, you keep this number in your call sign. This is also true should you upgrade to a higher license and get a new call sign. The numeral portion of your call sign stays the same.

Call Sign Numbers

Below is a chart showing the various numbers and the state(s) in which you would obtain the number.

Call Sign Number	State(s)
0	CO, IA, KS, MN, MO, NE, ND, SD
1	CT, ME, MA, NH, RI, VT
2	NJ, NY
3	DE, DC, MD, PA
4	AL, FL, GA, KY, NC, SC, TN, VA
5	AR, LA, MS, NM, OK, TX
6	CA
7	AZ, ID, MT, NV, OR, WA, UT, WY
8	MI, OH, WV
9	IL, IN, WI

Residents of Alaska may have any of the following call sign prefixes assigned to them: AL0-7, KL0-7, NL0-7, or WL0-7. Likewise, residents of Hawaii may have the prefix AH6-7, KH6-7, NH6-7, or WH6-7 assigned.

Once you obtain your Technician license, do not stop there. Go and get your General license.

General is the second of three ham license classes. Like the Technician license, to get a General license, you merely have to take a 35-question multiple choice exam and pay your license fee. Passing is still at least 26 correct answers and the fee is the same (less than $20). Again the question pool is available for free online (http://www.ncvec.org/page.php?id=358). It is also available in such print publications as *The ARRL General Class License Manual 7th Edition* (ISBN 978-0-87259-811-9). The current General pool of questions is to be used from July 1, 2011 to June 30, 2015. Be sure the question pool you are using is current. Being a bit more comprehensive than the Technician license, the General license usually requires 15-20 hours of study to learn the material. Check Appendix A for a listing of clubs in South Dakota where you might take your exam. Once your name and NEW call sign is listed in the FCC database, you're good to go. For a General license in South Dakota, your call sign will consist of a one-letter prefix beginning with K, N or W, the number zero (0), and a three-letter suffix.

Topics for the General License in Amateur Radio

The General license exam covers regulations, operating practices and electronic theory. Below is the syllabus for the General Class.

Subelement G1 – Commission's Rules
(5 Exam Questions – 5 Groups)
G1A – General Class control operator frequency privileges; primary and secondary allocations
G1B – Antenna structure limitations; good engineering and good amateur practice, beacon operation; restricted operation; retransmitting radio signals
G1C – Transmitter power regulations; data emission standards
G1D – Volunteer Examiners and Volunteer Examiner Coordinators; temporary identification
G1E – Control categories; repeater regulations; harmful interference; third party rules; ITU regions

Subelement G2 – Operating procedures
(5 Exam Questions – 5 Groups)
G2A – Phone operating procedures; USB/LSB utilization conventions; procedural signals; breaking into a OSO in progress; VOX operation
G2B – Operating courtesy; band plans, emergencies, including drills and emergency communications

G2C – CW operating procedures and procedural signals; Q signals and common abbreviations; full break in

G2D – Amateur Auxiliary; minimizing interference; HF operations

G2E – Digital operating; procedures, procedural signals and common abbreviations

Subelement G3 – Radio wave propagation

(3 Exam Questions – 3 Groups)

G3A – Sunspots and solar radiation; ionospheric disturbances; propagation forecasting and indices

G3B – Maximum Usable Frequency; Lowest Usable Frequency; propagation

G3C – Ionospheric layers; critical angle and frequency; HF scatter; Near Vertical Incidence Sky waves

Subelement G4 – Amateur radio practices

(5 Exam Questions – 5 Groups)

G4A – Station Operation and setup

G4B – Test and monitoring equipment; two-tone test

G4C – Interference with consumer electronics; grounding; DSP

G4D – Speech processors; S meters; sideband operation near band edges

G4E – HF mobile radio installations; emergency and battery powered operation

Subelement G5 – Electrical principles

(3 Exam Questions – 3 Groups)

G5A – Reactance; inductance; capacitance; impedance; impedance matching

G5B – The Decibel; current and voltage dividers; electrical power calculations; sine wave root-mean-square (RMS) values; PEP calculations

G5C – Resistors; capacitors and inductors in series and parallel; transformers

Subelement G6 – Circuit components

(3 Exam Questions – 3 Groups)

G6A – Resistors; capacitors; inductors

G6B – Rectifiers; solid state diodes and transistors; vacuum tubes; batteries

G6C – Analog and digital integrated circuits (ICs); microprocessors; memory; I/O devices; microwave ICs (MMICs); display devices

Subelement G7 – Practical circuits

(3 Exam Questions – 3 Groups)

G7A – Power supplies; schematic symbols

G7B – Digital circuits; amplifiers and oscillators

G7C – Receivers and transmitters; filters, oscillators

Subelement G8 – Signals and emissions

(2 Exam Questions – 2 Groups)

G8A – Carriers and modulation; AM; FM; single and double sideband; modulation envelope; overmodulation

G8B – Frequency mixing; multiplication; HF data communications; bandwidths of various modes; deviation

Subelement G9 – Antennas and feed lines

(4 Exam Questions – 4 Groups)

G9A – Antenna feed lines; characteristic impedance and attenuation; SWR calculation, measurement and effects; matching networks

G9B – Basic antennas

G9C – Directional antennas

G9D – Specialized antennas

Subelement G0 – Electrical and RF safety

(2 Exam Questions – 2 Groups)

G0A – RF safety principles, rules and guidelines; routine station elevation

G0B – Safety in the ham shack; electrical shock and treatment, safety grounding, fusing, interlocks, wiring, antenna and tower safety

With a General license, you can use all VHF and UHF frequencies and most of the HF frequencies. You would have access to the 160, 30, 17, 12, and 10 meter bands and access to major parts of the 80, 40, 20, and 15 meter bands. Of course, this is in addition to all bands available to Technician license holders.

Amateur Extra is the third of three ham license classes. Like the Technician and General classes, you merely have to pass a test and pay your fee to get your Amateur Extra license. This class of license is more comprehensive than the lower license classes. The exam is longer – 50 questions – and the minimum passing score is higher – 37. However, once you get your Amateur Extra license, all ham frequencies, VHF, UHF and HF are available for your enjoyment. The Extra exam covers regulations, specialized operating practices, advanced electronics theory, and radio equipment design.

Like for the other license classes, the question pool for the Amateur Extra license is available online for downloading (http://www.ncvec.org/downloads/REVISED%202012-2016%20Extra%20Class%20Pool.doc). It is also available in print form in such publications as *The ARRL Extra Class License Manual Revised 9th Edition* (ISBN 978-0-87259-887-4).

Topics for the Extra License in Amateur Radio

Below is the syllabus for the Amateur Extra Class for July 1, 2012 to June 30, 2016.

Subelement E1 – Commission's Rules

[6 Exam Questions – 6 Groups]

E1A – Operating Standards: frequency privileges; emission standards; automatic message forwarding; frequency sharing; stations aboard ships or aircraft

E1B – Station restrictions and special operations: restrictions on station location; general operating restrictions, spurious emissions, control operator reimbursement; antenna structure restrictions; RACES operations

E1C – Station control: definitions and restrictions pertaining to local, automatic and remote control operation; control operator responsibilities for remote and automatically controlled stations

E1D – Amateur Satellite service: definitions and purpose; license requirements for space stations; available frequencies and bands; telecommand and telemetry operations; restrictions, and special provisions; notification requirements

E1E – Volunteer examiner program: definitions, qualifications, preparation and administration of exams; accreditation; question pools; documentation requirements

E1F – Miscellaneous rules: external RF power amplifiers; national quiet zone; business communications; compensated communications; spread spectrum; auxiliary stations; reciprocal operating privileges; IARP and CEPT licenses; third party communications with foreign countries; special temporary authority

Subelement E2 – Operating procedures

[5 Exam Questions – 5 Groups]

E2A – Amateur radio in space: amateur satellites; orbital mechanics; frequencies and modes; satellite hardware; satellite operations

E2B – Television practices: fast scan television standards and techniques; slow scan television standards and techniques

E2C – Operating methods: contest and DX operating; spread-spectrum transmissions; selecting an operating frequency

E2D – Operating methods: VHF and UHF digital modes; APRS

E2E – Operating methods: operating HF digital modes; error correction

Subelement E3 – Radio wave propagation

[3 Exam Questions – 3 Groups]

E3A – Propagation and technique, Earth-Moon-Earth communications; meteor scatter

E3B – Propagation and technique, trans-equatorial; long path; gray-line; multi-path propagation

E3C – Propagation and technique, Aurora propagation; selective fading; radio-path horizon; take-off angle over flat or sloping terrain; effects of ground on propagation; less common propagation modes

Subelement E4 – Amateur practices

[5 Exam Questions – 5 Groups]

E4A – Test equipment: analog and digital instruments; spectrum and network analyzers, antenna analyzers; oscilloscopes; testing transistors; RF measurements

E4B – Measurement technique and limitations: instrument accuracy and performance limitations; probes; techniques to minimize errors; measurement of "Q"; instrument calibration

E4C – Receiver performance characteristics, phase noise, capture effect, noise floor, image rejection, MDS, signal-to-noise-ratio; selectivity

E4D – Receiver performance characteristics, blocking dynamic range, intermodulation and cross-modulation interference; 3rd order intercept; desensitization; preselection

E4E – Noise suppression: system noise; electrical appliance noise; line noise; locating noise sources; DSP noise reduction; noise blankers

Subelement E5 – Electrical principles

[4 Exam Questions – 4 Groups]

E5A – Resonance and Q: characteristics of resonant circuits: series and parallel resonance; Q; half-power bandwidth; phase relationships in reactive circuits

E5B – Time constants and phase relationships: RLC time constants: definition; time constants in RL and RC circuits; phase angle between voltage and current; phase angles of series and parallel circuits

E5C – Impedance plots and coordinate systems: plotting impedances in polar coordinates; rectangular coordinates

E5D – AC and RF energy in real circuits: skin effect; electrostatic and electromagnetic fields; reactive power; power factor; coordinate systems

Subelement E6 – Circuit components

[6 Exam Questions – 6 Groups]

E6A – Semiconductor materials and devices: semiconductor materials germanium, silicon, P-type, N-type; transistor types: NPN, PNP, junction, field-effect transistors: enhancement mode; depletion mode; MOS; CMOS; N-channel; P-channel

E6B – Semiconductor diodes

E6C – Integrated circuits: TTL digital integrated circuits; CMOS digital integrated circuits; gates

E6D – Optical devices and toroids: cathode-ray tube devices; charge-coupled devices (CCDs); liquid crystal displays (LCDs); toroids: permeability, core material, selecting, winding

E6E – Piezoelectric crystals and MMICs: quartz crystals; crystal oscillators and filters; monolithic amplifiers

E6F – Optical components and power systems: photoconductive principles and effects, photovoltaic systems, optical couplers, optical sensors, and optoisolators

Subelement E7 – Practical circuits

[8 Exam Questions – 8 Groups]

E7A – Digital circuits: digital circuit principles and logic circuits: classes of logic elements; positive and negative logic; frequency dividers; truth tables

E7B – Amplifiers: Class of operation; vacuum tube and solid-state circuits; distortion and intermodulation; spurious and parasitic suppression; microwave amplifiers

E7C – Filters and matching networks: filters and impedance matching networks: types of networks; types of filters; filter applications; filter characteristics; impedance matching; DSP filtering

E7D – Power supplies and voltage regulators

E7E – Modulation and demodulation: reactance, phase and balanced modulators; detectors; mixer stages; DSP modulation and demodulation; software defined radio systems

E7F – Frequency markers and counters: frequency divider circuits; frequency marker generators; frequency counters

E7G – Active filters and op-amps: active audio filters; characteristics; basic circuit design; operational amplifiers

E7H – Oscillators and signal sources: types of oscillators; synthesizers and phase-locked loops; direct digital synthesizers

Subelement E8 – Signals and emissions

[4 Exam Questions – 4 Groups]

E8A – AC waveforms: sine, square, sawtooth and irregular waveforms; AC measurements; average and PEP of RF signals; pulse and digital signal waveforms

E8B – Modulation and demodulation: modulation methods; modulation index and deviation ratio; pulse modulation; frequency and time division multiplexing

E8C – Digital signals: digital communications modes; CW; information rate vs. bandwidth; spread-spectrum communications; modulation methods

E8D – Waves, measurements, and RF grounding: peak-to-peak values, polarization; RF grounding

Subelement E9 – Antennas and transmission lines

[8 Exam Questions – 8 Groups]

E9A – Isotropic and gain antennas: definition; used as a standard for comparison; radiation pattern; basic antenna parameters: radiation resistance and reactance, gain, beamwidth, efficiency

E9B – Antenna patterns: E and H plane patterns; gain as a function of pattern; antenna design; Yagi antennas

E9C – Wire and phased vertical antennas: beverage antennas; terminated and resonant rhombic antennas; elevation above real ground; ground effects as related to polarization; take-off angles

E9D – Directional antennas: gain; satellite antennas; antenna beamwidth; losses; SWR bandwidth; antenna efficiency; shortened and mobile antennas; grounding

E9E – Matching: matching antennas to feed lines; power dividers

E9F – Transmission lines: characteristics of open and shorted feed lines: 1/8 wavelength; 1/4 wavelength; 1/2 wavelength; feed lines: coax versus open-wire; velocity factor; electrical length; transformation characteristics of line terminated in impedance not equal to characteristic impedance

E9G – The Smith chart

E9H – Effective radiated power; system gains and losses; radio direction finding antennas

[1 exam question – 1 group]
E0A – Safety: amateur radio safety practices; RF radiation hazards; hazardous materials

Once your new call sign is listed in the FCC database, you are good to go. For an Amateur Extra license in South Dakota, your call sign will consist of a prefix of K, N or W, the number zero (0), and a two-letter suffix, or a two-letter prefix beginning with A, N, K or W, the number zero (0), and a one-letter suffix, or a two-letter prefix beginning with A, the number zero (0), and a two-letter suffix.

Ham radio equipment can be expensive or you can do it "on the cheap." The cost will run from a couple hundred dollars to well in the thousands, depending on what you have available. eBay, and Craigslist are good places to start looking. Most ham clubs do some sort of hamfest annually wherein club members or others are willing to part with older equipment. See Appendix A for a list of clubs in South Dakota.

Another excellent source of equipment, as well as advice on setting the equipment up and how to use it properly, is current ham operators. In Appendix B, the author has listed all the FCC licensed ham operators in South Dakota, listed by city, and then sorted by street and house number on the street. Who knows, maybe someone who lives close to you is a ham operator. Be a good neighbor, stop by and have a chat with him/her.

Like CB radios, ham radios come in three formats – base, mobile, and handheld. They can use the electric company for power, or operate off a car battery. In the opinion of this author, in spite of the slightly higher cost of the equipment and having to take a test to legally use the equipment, ham radio is the way to go when concerned about communication during times of crisis.

Canadian Call Sign Prefixes

Because of our proximity to Canada, many times ham contact is made with our northern neighbors. Below is a chart showing the origin of Canadian call sign prefixes.

Call Sign Prefix	Provence or Territory
CY0	Sable Island
CY9	St. Paul Island
VA1, VE1	New Brunswick, Nova Scotia
VA2, VE2	Quebec
VA3, VE3	Ontario
VA4, VE4	Manitoba
VA5, VE5	Saskatchewan
VA6, VE6	Alberta
VA7, VE7	British Columbia
VE8	North West Territories
VE9	New Brunswick
VO1	Newfoundland

VO2	Labrador
VY0	Nunavut
VY1	Yukon
VY2	Prince Edward Island

Common Radio Bands in the United States

Certain radio bands are more popular with ham radio enthusiasts than others. Below is a chart showing these bands and when they are most popular.

	Band (meter)	Frequency (MHz)	Use
HF	160	1.8 – 2.0	Night
	80	3.5 – 4.0	Night and Local Day
	40	7.0 – 7.3	Night and Local Day
	30	10.1 – 10.15	CW and Digital
	20	14.0 – 14.350	World Wide Day and Night
	17	18.068 – 18.168	World Wide Day and Night
	15	21.0 – 21.450	Primarily Daytime
	12	24.890 – 24.990	Primarily Daytime
	10	28.0 – 29.70	Daytime during Sunspot highs
VHF	6	50 – 54	Local to World Wide
	2	144 – 148	Local to Medium Distance
UHF	70 cm	430 – 440	Local

Common Amateur Radio Bands in Canada

160 Meter Band - Maximum bandwidth 6 kHz
1.800 - 1.820 MHz - CW
1.820 - 1.830 MHz - Digital Modes
1 830 - 1.840 MHz - DX Window
1.840 - 2.000 MHz - SSB and other wide band modes

80 Meter Band - Maximum bandwidth 6 kHz
3.500 - 3.580 MHz - CW
3.580 - 3.620 MHz - Digital Modes
3.620 - 3.635 MHz - Packet/Digital Secondary
3.635 - 3.725 MHz - CW
3.725 - 3.790 MHz - SSB and other side band modes*
3.790 - 3.800 MHz - SSB DX Window
3.800 - 4.000 MHz - SSB and other wide band modes

40 Meter Band - Maximum bandwidth 6 kHz
7.000 - 7.035 MHz - CW
7.035 - 7.050 MHz - Digital Modes
7.040 - 7.050 MHz - International packet

7.050 - 7.100 MHz - SSB
7.100 - 7.120 MHz - Packet within Region 2
7.120 - 7.150 MHz - CW
7.150 - 7.300 MHz - SSB and other wide band modes

30 Meter Band - Maximum bandwidth 1 kHz

10.100 - 10.130 MHz - CW only
10.130 - 10.140 MHz - Digital Modes
10.140 - 10.150 MHz - Packet

20 Meter Band - Maximum bandwidth 6 kHz

14.000 - 14.070 MHz - CW only
14.070 - 14.095 MHz - Digital Mode
14.095 - 14.099 MHz - Packet
14.100 MHz - Beacons
14.101 - 14.112 MHz - CW, SSB, packet shared
14.112 - 14.350 MHz - SSB
14.225 - 14.235 MHz - SSTV

17 Meter Band - Maximum bandwidth 6 kHz

18.068 - 18.100 MHz - CW
18.100 - 18.105 MHz - Digital Modes
18.105 - 18.110 MHz - Packet
18.110 - 18.168 MHz - SSB and other wide band modes

15 Meter Band - maximum bandwidth 6 kHz

21.000 - 21.070 MHz - CW
21.070 - 21.090 MHz - Digital Modes
21.090 - 21.125 MHz - Packet
21.100 - 21.150 MHz - CW and SSB
21.150 - 21.335 MHz - SSB and other wide band modes
21.335 - 21.345 MHz - SSTV
21.345 - 21.450 MHz - SSB and other wide band modes

12 Meter Band - Maximum bandwidth 6 kHz

24.890 - 24.930 MHz - CW
24.920 - 24.925 MHz - Digital Modes
24.925 - 24.930 MHz - Packet
24.930 - 24.990 MHz - SSB and other wide band modes

10 Meter Band - Maximum band width 20 kHz

28.000 - 28.200 MHz - CW
28.070 - 28.120 MHz - Digital Modes
28.120 - 28.190 MHz - Packet

28.190 - 28.200 MHz - Beacons
28.200 - 29.300 MHz - SSB and other wide band modes
29.300 - 29.510 MHz - Satellite
29.510 - 29.700 MHz - SSB, FM and repeaters

160 Meters (1.8-2.0 MHz)

1.800 - 2.000 CW
1.800 - 1.810 Digital Modes
1.810 CW QRP
1.843-2.000 SSB, SSTV and other wideband modes
1.910 SSB QRP
1.995 - 2.000 Experimental
1.999 - 2.000 Beacons

80 Meters (3.5-4.0 MHz)

3.590 RTTY/Data DX
3.570-3.600 RTTY/Data
3.790-3.800 DX window
3.845 SSTV
3.885 AM calling frequency

40 Meters (7.0-7.3 MHz)

7.040 RTTY/Data DX
7.080-7.125 RTTY/Data
7.171 SSTV
7.290 AM calling frequency

30 Meters (10.1-10.15 MHz)

10.130-10.140 RTTY
10.140-10.150 Packet

20 Meters (14.0-14.35 MHz)

14.070-14.095 RTTY
14.095-14.0995 Packet
14.100 NCDXF Beacons
14.1005-14.112 Packet
14.230 SSTV
14.286 AM calling frequency

17 Meters (18.068-18.168 MHz)

18.100-18.105 RTTY
18.105-18.110 Packet

15 Meters (21.0-21.45 MHz)

21.070-21.110 RTTY/Data

21.340 SSTV

12 Meters (24.89-24.99 MHz)
24.920-24.925 RTTY
24.925-24.930 Packet

10 Meters (28-29.7 MHz)
28.000-28.070 CW
28.070-28.150 RTTY
28.150-28.190 CW
28.200-28.300 Beacons
28.300-29.300 Phone
28.680 SSTV
29.000-29.200 AM
29.300-29.510 Satellite Downlinks
29.520-29.590 Repeater Inputs
29.600 FM Simplex
29.610-29.700 Repeater Outputs

6 Meters (50-54 MHz)
50.0-50.1 CW, beacons
50.060-50.080 beacon subband
50.1-50.3 SSB, CW
50.10-50.125 DX window
50.125 SSB calling
50.3-50.6 All modes
50.6-50.8 Nonvoice communications
50.62 Digital (packet) calling
50.8-51.0 Radio remote control (20-kHz channels)
51.0-51.1 Pacific DX window
51.12-51.48 Repeater inputs (19 channels)
51.12-51.18 Digital repeater inputs
51.5-51.6 Simplex (seven channels)
51.62-51.98 Repeater outputs (19 channels)
51.62-51.68 Digital repeater outputs
52.0-52.48 Repeater inputs (except as noted; 23 channels)
52.02, 52.04 FM simplex
52.2 TEST PAIR (input)
52.5-52.98 Repeater output (except as noted; 23 channels)
52.525 Primary FM simplex
52.54 Secondary FM simplex
52.7 TEST PAIR (output)
53.0-53.48 Repeater inputs (except as noted; 19 channels)
53.0 Remote base FM simplex
53.02 Simplex
53.1, 53.2, 53.3, 53.4 Radio remote control

53.5-53.98 Repeater outputs (except as noted; 19 channels)
53.5, 53.6, 53.7, 53.8 Radio remote control
53.52, 53.9 Simplex

2 Meters (144-148 MHz)

144.00-144.05 EME (CW)
144.05-144.10 General CW and weak signals
144.10-144.20 EME and weak-signal SSB
144.200 National calling frequency
144.200-144.275 General SSB operation
144.275-144.300 Propagation beacons
144.30-144.50 New OSCAR subband
144.50-144.60 Linear translator inputs
144.60-144.90 FM repeater inputs
144.90-145.10 Weak signal and FM simplex (145.01,03,05,07,09 are widely used for packet)
145.10-145.20 Linear translator outputs
145.20-145.50 FM repeater outputs
145.50-145.80 Miscellaneous and experimental modes
145.80-146.00 OSCAR subband
146.01-146.37 Repeater inputs
146.40-146.58 Simplex
146.52 National Simplex Calling Frequency
146.61-146.97 Repeater outputs
147.00-147.39 Repeater outputs
147.42-147.57 Simplex
147.60-147.99 Repeater inputs

1.25 Meters (222-225 MHz)

222.0-222.150 Weak-signal modes
222.0-222.025 EME
222.05-222.06 Propagation beacons
222.1 SSB & CW calling frequency
222.10-222.15 Weak-signal CW & SSB
222.15-222.25 Local coordinator's option; weak signal, ACSB, repeater inputs, control
222.25-223.38 FM repeater inputs only
223.40-223.52 FM simplex
223.52-223.64 Digital, packet
223.64-223.70 Links, control
223.71-223.85 Local coordinator's option; FM simplex, packet, repeater outputs
223.85-224.98 Repeater outputs only

70 Centimeters (420-450 MHz)

420.00-426.00 ATV repeater or simplex with 421.25 MHz video carrier control links and experimental

426.00-432.00 ATV simplex with 427.250-MHz video carrier frequency
432.00-432.07 EME (Earth-Moon-Earth)
432.07-432.10 Weak-signal CW
432.10 70-cm calling frequency
432.10-432.30 Mixed-mode and weak-signal work
432.30-432.40 Propagation beacons
432.40-433.00 Mixed-mode and weak-signal work
433.00-435.00 Auxiliary/repeater links
435.00-438.00 Satellite only (internationally)
438.00-444.00 ATV repeater input with 439.250-MHz video carrier frequency and repeater links
442.00-445.00 Repeater inputs and outputs (local option)
445.00-447.00 Shared by auxiliary and control links, repeaters and simplex (local option)
446.00 National simplex frequency
447.00-450.00 Repeater inputs and outputs (local option)

33 Centimeters (902-928 MHz)

902.0-903.0 Narrow-bandwidth, weak-signal communications
902.0-902.8 SSTV, FAX, ACSSB, experimental
902.1 Weak-signal calling frequency
902.8-903.0 Reserved for EME, CW expansion
903.1 Alternate calling frequency
903.0-906.0 Digital communications
906-909 FM repeater inputs
909-915 ATV
915-918 Digital communications
918-921 FM repeater outputs
921-927 ATV
927-928 FM simplex and links

23 Centimeters (1240-1300 MHz)

1240-1246 ATV #1
1246-1248 Narrow-bandwidth FM point-to-point links and digital, duplex with 1258-1260.
1248-1258 Digital Communications
1252-1258 ATV #2
1258-1260 Narrow-bandwidth FM point-to-point links digital, duplexed with 1246-1252
1260-1270 Satellite uplinks, reference WARC '79
1260-1270 Wide-bandwidth experimental, simplex ATV
1270-1276 Repeater inputs, FM and linear, paired with 1282-1288, 239 pairs every 25 kHz, e.g. 1270.025, .050, etc.
1271-1283 Non-coordinated test pair
1276-1282 ATV #3
1282-1288 Repeater outputs, paired with 1270-1276
1288-1294 Wide-bandwidth experimental, simplex ATV
1294-1295 Narrow-bandwidth FM simplex services, 25-kHz channels

1294.5 National FM simplex calling frequency
1295-1297 Narrow bandwidth weak-signal communications (no FM)
1295.0-1295.8 SSTV, FAX, ACSSB, experimental
1295.8-1296.0 Reserved for EME, CW expansion
1296.00-1296.05 EME-exclusive
1296.07-1296.08 CW beacons
1296.1 CW, SSB calling frequency
1296.4-1296.6 Crossband linear translator input
1296.6-1296.8 Crossband linear translator output
1296.8-1297.0 Experimental beacons (exclusive)
1297-1300 Digital Communications

2300-2310 and 2390-2450 MHz

2300.0-2303.0 High-rate data
2303.0-2303.5 Packet
2303.5-2303.8 TTY packet
2303.9-2303.9 Packet, TTY, CW, EME
2303.9-2304.1 CW, EME
2304.1 Calling frequency
2304.1-2304.2 CW, EME, SSB
2304.2-2304.3 SSB, SSTV, FAX, Packet AM, Amtor
2304.30-2304.32 Propagation beacon network
2304.32-2304.40 General propagation beacons
2304.4-2304.5 SSB, SSTV, ACSSB, FAX, Packet AM, Amtor experimental
2304.5-2304.7 Crossband linear translator input
2304.7-2304.9 Crossband linear translator output
2304.9-2305.0 Experimental beacons
2305.0-2305.2 FM simplex (25 kHz spacing)
2305.20 FM simplex calling frequency
2305.2-2306.0 FM simplex (25 kHz spacing)
2306.0-2309.0 FM Repeaters (25 kHz) input
2309.0-2310.0 Control and auxiliary links
2390.0-2396.0 Fast-scan TV
2396.0-2399.0 High-rate data
2399.0-2399.5 Packet
2399.5-2400.0 Control and auxiliary links
2400.0-2403.0 Satellite
2403.0-2408.0 Satellite high-rate data
2408.0-2410.0 Satellite
2410.0-2413.0 FM repeaters (25 kHz) output
2413.0-2418.0 High-rate data
2418.0-2430.0 Fast-scan TV
2430.0-2433.0 Satellite
2433.0-2438.0 Satellite high-rate data
2438.0-2450.0 WB FM, FSTV, FMTV, SS experimental

3300-3500 MHz
3456.3-3456.4 Propagation beacons

5650-5925 MHz
5760.3-5760.4 Propagation beacons

10.00-10.50 GHz
10.368 Narrow band calling frequency 10.3683-10.3684 Propagation beacons 10.3640 Calling frequency

Now that you have your license (you do, don't you?), and your equipment, you are ready to go live. Below is a suggested start.

1) Assuming you have the HT set up to the appropriate frequency, and offset, press the mic button on the HT and say, "KK4HWX listening." Replace the KK4HWX with your own call sign, the one assigned to you by the FCC (it's the law). If no one responds to your call, you may wish to try again. Hopefully someone will respond to your call.

2) Once you get a response, it will be in the form of something like, "KK4HWX this is ??1??? in Eastport returning. My name is Florence. Back to you. ??1???" then a tone. Let us examine the response more closely. She first acknowledged your call sign (KK4HWX), then identified hers (??1???). From the 1 in her call sign, you know that she first got her license in Region 1, meaning she got it while a resident of CT, ME, MA, NH, RI, or VT. She then told you where she's transmitting from (Eastport). The term "returning" means that she is returning your call. Her name is Florence. The phrase, "Back to you" indicates that she is turning over the conversation to you. She then repeats her call sign. The tone indicates to you that it is okay to proceed with your response. BTW if she had used the term "Over" instead of "Back to you," it would mean the same thing, just fewer words.

3) At this point, press the mic button and continue with the conversation. You should restate your call sign often during the conversation (perhaps every 10 minutes or less and whenever you begin transmitting). Don't forget to say, "Over" or "Back to you" whenever you are giving Florence control of the conversation again.

4) When you are ready to stop the conversation, you should say goodbye or use the phrase "73", meaning "best wishes." Your conversation would end something like, "??1??? 73, this is KK4HWX clear and monitoring." The "clear and monitoring" indicates that you are going to continue to monitor the frequency. If you are not going to continue monitoring, you may wish to end the conversation with Florence with, "clear and QRT" instead. The QRT means that you are stopping transmissions.

Call Sign Phonics

Because of different accents of various people, sometimes it is difficult to understand call sign letters when spoken. For this reason, most ham operators verbalize their call sign using phonics. Below is a table listing the accepted phonics for letters and numbers.

A = ALFA   S = SIERRA
B = BRAVO   T = TANGO
C = CHARLIE   U = UNIFORM
D = DELTA   V = VICTOR
E = ECHO   W = WHISKEY
F = FOXTROT   X = X-RAY
G = GOLF   Y = YANKEE
H = HOTEL   Z = ZULU (ZED)
I = INDIA   1 = ONE
J = JULIETT   2 = TWO
K = KILO   3 = THREE (TREE)
L = LIMA   4 = FOUR
M = MIKE   5 = FIVE (FIFE)
N = NOVEMBER   6 = SEVEN
O = OSCAR   7 = SEVEN
P = PAPA (PA-PA')   8 = EIGHT
Q = QUEBEC (KAY-BEK')   9 = NINE (NINER)
R = ROMEO   0 = ZERO

The words in parentheses are the pronunciation or the alternate pronunciations for the words or numbers, but you will hear both used. With the letter Z, (ZED) is by far the most commonly used. With the number 9, NINER is the most common and easiest to understand ON THE AIR.

If you wish to use Morse code (CW) instead of voice communication, the "conversation" would follow the same steps, with a few modifications. To type out each word would require a lot of typing and translating. If you are like this author, more means more, i.e., more typing means more typos are likely. To help with this situation, CW enthusiasts have developed a language all their own – they use abbreviations for common phrases. Below is a chart showing some of these abbreviations.

Abbreviation	Use
AR	Over
de	From or "this is"
ES	And
GM	Good Morning
K	Go
KN	Go only
NM	Name
QTH	Location
RPT	Report
R	Roger
SK	Clear

tnx	Thanks
UR	Your, you are
73	Best Wishes

Morse Code and Amateur Radio

If you wish to use CW, but are concerned about accuracy, you might consider purchasing a Morse code translator. This is an electronic device that you place in front of your speakers. It takes the CW sounds and translates them into English and displays the transmission on an LCD display. For the reverse, you can pick up a CW keyboard. With the keyboard, you type in your message and it converts the text to Morse code. The translator does not need to be attached to your ham equipment, whereas the keyboard would.

For your convenience, below is a table showing the Morse code signals and their meaning.

Character	Code
A	· —
B	— · · ·
C	— · — ·
D	— · ·
E	·
F	· · — ·
G	— — ·
H	· · · ·
I	· ·
J	· — — —
K	— · —
L	· — · ·
M	— —
N	— ·
O	— — —
P	· — — ·
Q	— — · —
R	· — ·
S	· · ·
T	—
U	· · —
V	· · · —
W	· — —
X	— · · —
Y	— · — —
Z	— — · ·
0	— — — — —
1	· — — — —

2	· · — — —
3	· · · — —
4	· · · · —
5	· · · · ·
6	— · · · ·
7	— — · · ·
8	— — — · ·
9	— — — — ·
Ampersand [&], Wait	· — · · ·
Apostrophe [']	· — — — — ·
At sign [@]	· — — · — ·
Colon [:]	— — — · · ·
Comma [,]	— — · · — —
Dollar sign [$]	· · · — · · —
Double dash [=]	— · · · —
Exclamation mark [!]	— · — · — —
Hyphen, Minus [-]	— · · · · —
Parenthesis closed [)]	— · — — · —
Parenthesis open [(]	— · — — ·
Period [.]	· — · — · —
Plus [+]	· — · — ·
Question mark [?]	· · — — · ·
Quotation mark ["]	· — · · — ·
Semicolon [;]	— · — · — ·
Slash [/], Fraction bar	— · · — ·
Underscore [_]	· · — — · —

An advantage of using Morse Code is that when broadcasting CW, you are using reduced power, thereby saving your battery. Your battery is used only while actually transmitting or receiving.

International Call Sign Prefixes

As was stated earlier, all ham radio call signs begin with letters (or numbers) taken from blocks assigned to each country of the world by the *ITU - International Telecommunications Union,* a body controlled by the United Nations. The following chart indicates which call sign series are allocated to which countries.

Call Sign Series	Allocated to
AAA-ALZ	**United States of America**
AMA-AOZ	Spain
APA-ASZ	Pakistan (Islamic Republic of)
ATA-AWZ	India (Republic of)
AXA-AXZ	Australia
AYA-AZZ	Argentine Republic

A2A-A2Z	Botswana (Republic of)
A3A-A3Z	Tonga (Kingdom of)
A4A-A4Z	Oman (Sultanate of)
A5A-A5Z	Bhutan (Kingdom of)
A6A-A6Z	United Arab Emirates
A7A-A7Z	Qatar (State of)
A8A-A8Z	Liberia (Republic of)
A9A-A9Z	Bahrain (State of)
BAA-BZZ	China (People's Republic of)
CAA-CEZ	Chile
CFA-CKZ	Canada
CLA-CMZ	Cuba
CNA-CNZ	Morocco (Kingdom of)
COA-COZ	Cuba
CPA-CPZ	Bolivia (Republic of)
CQA-CUZ	Portugal
CVA-CXZ	Uruguay (Eastern Republic of)
CYA-CZZ	Canada
C2A-C2Z	Nauru (Republic of)
C3A-C3Z	Andorra (Principality of)
C4A-C4Z	Cyprus (Republic of)
C5A-C5Z	Gambia (Republic of the)
C6A-C6Z	Bahamas (Commonwealth of the)
C7A-C7Z	World Meteorological Organization
C8A-C9Z	Mozambique (Republic of)
DAA-DRZ	Germany (Federal Republic of)
DSA-DTZ	Korea (Republic of)
DUA-DZZ	Philippines (Republic of the)
D2A-D3Z	Angola (Republic of)
D4A-D4Z	Cape Verde (Republic of)
D5A-D5Z	Liberia (Republic of)
D6A-D6Z	Comoros (Islamic Federal Republic of the)
D7A-D9Z	Korea (Republic of)
EAA-EHZ	Spain
EIA-EJZ	Ireland
EKA-EKZ	Armenia (Republic of)
ELA-ELZ	Liberia (Republic of)
EMA-EOZ	Ukraine
EPA-EQZ	Iran (Islamic Republic of)
ERA-ERZ	Moldova (Republic of)
ESA-ESZ	Estonia (Republic of)
ETA-ETZ	Ethiopia (Federal Democratic Republic of)
EUA-EWZ	Belarus (Republic of)
EXA-EXZ	Kyrgyz Republic
EYA-EYZ	Tajikistan (Republic of)

EZA-EZZ	Turkmenistan
E2A-E2Z	Thailand
E3A-E3Z	Eritrea
E4A-E4Z	Palestinian Authority
E5A-E5Z	New Zealand - Cook Islands (WRC-07)
E7A-E7Z	Bosnia and Herzegovina (Republic of) (WRC-07)
FAA-FZZ	France
GAA-GZZ	United Kingdom of Great Britain and Northern Ireland
HAA-HAZ	Hungary (Republic of)
HBA-HBZ	Switzerland (Confederation of)
HCA-HDZ	Ecuador
HEA-HEZ	Switzerland (Confederation of)
HFA-HFZ	Poland (Republic of)
HGA-HGZ	Hungary (Republic of)
HHA-HHZ	Haiti (Republic of)
HIA-HIZ	Dominican Republic
HJA-HKZ	Colombia (Republic of)
HLA-HLZ	Korea (Republic of)
HMA-HMZ	Democratic People's Republic of Korea
HNA-HNZ	Iraq (Republic of)
HOA-HPZ	Panama (Republic of)
HQA-HRZ	Honduras (Republic of)
HSA-HSZ	Thailand
HTA-HTZ	Nicaragua
HUA-HUZ	El Salvador (Republic of)
HVA-HVZ	Vatican City State
HWA-HYZ	France
HZA-HZZ	Saudi Arabia (Kingdom of)
H2A-H2Z	Cyprus (Republic of)
H3A-H3Z	Panama (Republic of)
H4A-H4Z	Solomon Islands
H6A-H7Z	Nicaragua
H8A-H9Z	Panama (Republic of)
IAA-IZZ	Italy
JAA-JSZ	Japan
JTA-JVZ	Mongolia
JWA-JXZ	Norway
JYA-JYZ	Jordan (Hashemite Kingdom of)
JZA-JZZ	Indonesia (Republic of)
J2A-J2Z	Djibouti (Republic of)
J3A-J3Z	Grenada
J4A-J4Z	Greece
J5A-J5Z	Guinea-Bissau (Republic of)
J6A-J6Z	Saint Lucia
J7A-J7Z	Dominica (Commonwealth of)

J8A-J8Z	Saint Vincent and the Grenadines
KAA-KZZ	**United States of America**
LAA-LNZ	Norway
LOA-LWZ	Argentine Republic
LXA-LXZ	Luxembourg
LYA-LYZ	Lithuania (Republic of)
LZA-LZZ	Bulgaria (Republic of)
L2A-L9Z	Argentine Republic
MAA-MZZ	United Kingdom of Great Britain and Northern Ireland
NAA-NZZ	**United States of America**
OAA-OCZ	Peru
ODA-ODZ	Lebanon
OEA-OEZ	Austria
OFA-OJZ	Finland
OKA-OLZ	Czech Republic
OMA-OMZ	Slovak Republic
ONA-OTZ	Belgium
OUA-OZZ	Denmark
PAA-PIZ	Netherlands (Kingdom of the)
PJA-PJZ	Netherlands (Kingdom of the) - Netherlands Antilles
PKA-POZ	Indonesia (Republic of)
PPA-PYZ	Brazil (Federative Republic of)
PZA-PZZ	Suriname (Republic of)
P2A-P2Z	Papua New Guinea
P3A-P3Z	Cyprus (Republic of)
P4A-P4Z	Netherlands (Kingdom of the) - Aruba
P5A-P9Z	Democratic People's Republic of Korea
RAA-RZZ	Russian Federation
SAA-SMZ	Sweden
SNA-SRZ	Poland (Republic of)
SSA-SSM	Egypt (Arab Republic of)
SSN-STZ	Sudan (Republic of the)
SUA-SUZ	Egypt (Arab Republic of)
SVA-SZZ	Greece
S2A-S3Z	Bangladesh (People's Republic of)
S5A-S5Z	Slovenia (Republic of)
S6A-S6Z	Singapore (Republic of)
S7A-S7Z	Seychelles (Republic of)
S8A-S8Z	South Africa (Republic of)
S9A-S9Z	Sao Tome and Principe (Democratic Republic of)
TAA-TCZ	Turkey
TDA-TDZ	Guatemala (Republic of)
TEA-TEZ	Costa Rica
TFA-TFZ	Iceland
TGA-TGZ	Guatemala (Republic of)

THA-THZ	France
TIA-TIZ	Costa Rica
TJA-TJZ	Cameroon (Republic of)
TKA-TKZ	France
TLA-TLZ	Central African Republic
TMA-TMZ	France
TNA-TNZ	Congo (Republic of the)
TOA-TQZ	France
TRA-TRZ	Gabonese Republic
TSA-TSZ	Tunisia
TTA-TTZ	Chad (Republic of)
TUA-TUZ	Côte d'Ivoire (Republic of)
TVA-TXZ	France
TYA-TYZ	Benin (Republic of)
TZA-TZZ	Mali (Republic of)
T2A-T2Z	Tuvalu
T3A-T3Z	Kiribati (Republic of)
T4A-T4Z	Cuba
T5A-T5Z	Somali Democratic Republic
T6A-T6Z	Afghanistan (Islamic State of)
T7A-T7Z	San Marino (Republic of)
T8A-T8Z	Palau (Republic of)
UAA-UIZ	Russian Federation
UJA-UMZ	Uzbekistan (Republic of)
UNA-UQZ	Kazakhstan (Republic of)
URA-UZZ	Ukraine
VAA-VGZ	Canada
VHA-VNZ	Australia
VOA-VOZ	Canada
VPA-VQZ	United Kingdom of Great Britain and Northern Ireland
VRA-VRZ	China (People's Republic of) - Hong Kong
VSA-VSZ	United Kingdom of Great Britain and Northern Ireland
VTA-VWZ	India (Republic of)
VXA-VYZ	Canada
VZA-VZZ	Australia
V2A-V2Z	Antigua and Barbuda
V3A-V3Z	Belize
V4A-V4Z	Saint Kitts and Nevis
V5A-V5Z	Namibia (Republic of)
V6A-V6Z	Micronesia (Federated States of)
V7A-V7Z	Marshall Islands (Republic of the)
V8A-V8Z	Brunei Darussalam
WAA-WZZ	**United States of America**
XAA-XIZ	Mexico
XJA-XOZ	Canada

XPA-XPZ	Denmark
XQA-XRZ	Chile
XSA-XSZ	China (People's Republic of)
XTA-XTZ	Burkina Faso
XUA-XUZ	Cambodia (Kingdom of)
XVA-XVZ	Viet Nam (Socialist Republic of)
XWA-XWZ	Lao People's Democratic Republic
XXA-XXZ	China (People's Republic of) - Macao (WRC-07)
XYA-XZZ	Myanmar (Union of)
YAA-YAZ	Afghanistan (Islamic State of)
YBA-YHZ	Indonesia (Republic of)
YIA-YIZ	Iraq (Republic of)
YJA-YJZ	Vanuatu (Republic of)
YKA-YKZ	Syrian Arab Republic
YLA-YLZ	Latvia (Republic of)
YMA-YMZ	Turkey
YNA-YNZ	Nicaragua
YOA-YRZ	Romania
YSA-YSZ	El Salvador (Republic of)
YTA-YUZ	Serbia (Republic of) (WRC-07)
YVA-YYZ	Venezuela (Republic of)
Y2A-Y9Z	Germany (Federal Republic of)
ZAA-ZAZ	Albania (Republic of)
ZBA-ZJZ	United Kingdom of Great Britain and Northern Ireland
ZKA-ZMZ	New Zealand
ZNA-ZOZ	United Kingdom of Great Britain and Northern Ireland
ZPA-ZPZ	Paraguay (Republic of)
ZQA-ZQZ	United Kingdom of Great Britain and Northern Ireland
ZRA-ZUZ	South Africa (Republic of)
ZVA-ZZZ	Brazil (Federative Republic of)
Z2A-Z2Z	Zimbabwe (Republic of)
Z3A-Z3Z	The Former Yugoslav Republic of Macedonia
2AA-2ZZ	United Kingdom of Great Britain and Northern Ireland
3AA-3AZ	Monaco (Principality of)
3BA-3BZ	Mauritius (Republic of)
3CA-3CZ	Equatorial Guinea (Republic of)
3DA-3DM	Swaziland (Kingdom of)
3DN-3DZ	Fiji (Republic of)
3EA-3FZ	Panama (Republic of)
3GA-3GZ	Chile
3HA-3UZ	China (People's Republic of)
3VA-3VZ	Tunisia
3WA-3WZ	Viet Nam (Socialist Republic of)
3XA-3XZ	Guinea (Republic of)
3YA-3YZ	Norway

3ZA-3ZZ	Poland (Republic of)
4AA-4CZ	Mexico
4DA-4IZ	Philippines (Republic of the)
4JA-4KZ	Azerbaijani Republic
4LA-4LZ	Georgia (Republic of)
4MA-4MZ	Venezuela (Republic of)
4OA-4OZ	Montenegro (Republic of) (WRC-07)
4PA-4SZ	Sri Lanka (Democratic Socialist Republic of)
4TA-4TZ	Peru
4UA-4UZ	United Nations
4VA-4VZ	Haiti (Republic of)
4WA-4WZ	Democratic Republic of Timor-Leste (WRC-03)
4XA-4XZ	Israel (State of)
4YA-4YZ	International Civil Aviation Organization
4ZA-4ZZ	Israel (State of)
5AA-5AZ	Libya (Socialist People's Libyan Arab Jamahiriya)
5BA-5BZ	Cyprus (Republic of)
5CA-5GZ	Morocco (Kingdom of)
5HA-5IZ	Tanzania (United Republic of)
5JA-5KZ	Colombia (Republic of)
5LA-5MZ	Liberia (Republic of)
5NA-5OZ	Nigeria (Federal Republic of)
5PA-5QZ	Denmark
5RA-5SZ	Madagascar (Republic of)
5TA-5TZ	Mauritania (Islamic Republic of)
5UA-5UZ	Niger (Republic of the)
5VA-5VZ	Togolese Republic
5WA-5WZ	Samoa (Independent State of)
5XA-5XZ	Uganda (Republic of)
5YA-5ZZ	Kenya (Republic of)
6AA-6BZ	Egypt (Arab Republic of)
6CA-6CZ	Syrian Arab Republic
6DA-6JZ	Mexico
6KA-6NZ	Korea (Republic of)
6OA-6OZ	Somali Democratic Republic
6PA-6SZ	Pakistan (Islamic Republic of)
6TA-6UZ	Sudan (Republic of the)
6VA-6WZ	Senegal (Republic of)
6XA-6XZ	Madagascar (Republic of)
6YA-6YZ	Jamaica
6ZA-6ZZ	Liberia (Republic of)
7AA-7IZ	Indonesia (Republic of)
7JA-7NZ	Japan
7OA-7OZ	Yemen (Republic of)
7PA-7PZ	Lesotho (Kingdom of)

7QA-7QZ	Malawi
7RA-7RZ	Algeria (People's Democratic Republic of)
7SA-7SZ	Sweden
7TA-7YZ	Algeria (People's Democratic Republic of)
7ZA-7ZZ	Saudi Arabia (Kingdom of)
8AA-8IZ	Indonesia (Republic of)
8JA-8NZ	Japan
8OA-8OZ	Botswana (Republic of)
8PA-8PZ	Barbados
8QA-8QZ	Maldives (Republic of)
8RA-8RZ	Guyana
8SA-8SZ	Sweden
8TA-8YZ	India (Republic of)
8ZA-8ZZ	Saudi Arabia (Kingdom of)
9AA-9AZ	Croatia (Republic of)
9BA-9DZ	Iran (Islamic Republic of)
9EA-9FZ	Ethiopia (Federal Democratic Republic of)
9GA-9GZ	Ghana
9HA-9HZ	Malta
9IA-9JZ	Zambia (Republic of)
9KA-9KZ	Kuwait (State of)
9LA-9LZ	Sierra Leone
9MA-9MZ	Malaysia
9NA-9NZ	Nepal
9OA-9TZ	Democratic Republic of the Congo
9UA-9UZ	Burundi (Republic of)
9VA-9VZ	Singapore (Republic of)
9WA-9WZ	Malaysia
9XA-9XZ	Rwandese Republic
9YA-9ZZ	Trinidad and Tobago

Third-Party Communications and Amateur Radio

If all of this information about ham radios is somewhat intimidating, do not despair. "You" can still use ham radios for communications without being a licensed operator. Yes, you do have to have a ham license in order to legally transmit by ham equipment (or be under the direct supervision of someone else who is licensed), but there is an alternative – third-party communication.

Third-party communications occur when a licensed operator sends either written or verbal messages on behalf of unlicensed persons or organizations. There are two "controls" on third-party communication.

First, the communication must be noncommercial and of a personal nature. Asking a ham operator to contact another ham operator located in an area just hit by tornados and, because of being without power, phones do not work in Grandma Sally's city so you can check up on her, is okay. Asking a ham to send a message out that you have an old Chevy for sale would not be okay.

Second, the message must be going to a permitted area. Transmitting from a US location to another US location is okay, but transmitting from the US to another country may not. Because third-party communications bypass a country's normal telephone and postal systems, many foreign governments forbid such communications. In order to transmit from one country to another, the other country must have signed a third-party agreement with the US. What follows is a list of those countries that do have third-party a communications agreement with the US.

V2	Antigua / Barbuda
LU	Argentina
VK	Australia
V3	Belize
CP	Bolivia
T9	Bosnia-Herzegovina
PY	Brazil
VE	Canada
CE	Chile
HK	Colombia
D6	Comoros (Federal Islamic Republic of)
TI	Costa Rica
CO	Cuba
HI	Dominican Republic
J7	Dominica
HC	Ecuador
YS	El Salvador
C5	Gambia, The
9G	Ghana
J3	Grenada
TG	Guatemala
8R	Guyana
HH	Haiti
HR	Honduras
4X	Israel
6Y	Jamaica
JY	Jordan
EL	Liberia
V7	Marshall Islands
XE	Mexico
V6	Micronesia, Federated States of
YN	Nicaragua
HP	Panama

ZP	Paraguay
OA	Peru
DU	Philippines
VR6	Pitcairn Island
V4	St. Christopher / Nevis
J6	St. Lucia
J8	St. Vincent and the Grenadines
9L	Sierra Leone
ZS	South Africa
3DA	Swaziland
9Y	Trinidad / Tobago
TA	Turkey
GB	United Kingdom
CX	Uruguay
YV	Venezuela
4U1ITUITU	Geneva
4U1VICVIC	Vienna

Remember, before TSHTF, keep your pantry well stocked, your powder dry, and your batteries fully charged. 73

APPENDIX A

American Radio Relay League

Affiliated Amateur Radio Clubs in

South Dakota

ARRL Affiliated Club	**Hub City Amateur Radio Club**
City:	Aberdeen, SD
Call Sign:	W0ABR
Section:	SD
Links:	www.w0abr.com

ARRL Affiliated Club	**Northern Hills Amateur Radio Club**
City:	Belle Fourche, SD
Call Sign:	KC0BXH
Section:	SD
Links:	www.northernhillsarc.org

ARRL Affiliated Club	**Radio Research Club Inc.**
City:	Elkton, SD
Call Sign:	W0BXO
Section:	SD

ARRL Special Service Club	**HOT SPRINGS Amateur Radio Club**
City:	Hot Springs, SD
Call Sign:	K0HS
Section:	SD

ARRL Affiliated Club	**Huron Amateur Radio Club Inc.**
City:	Huron, SD
Call Sign:	W0NOZ
Section:	SD
Links:	www.huronarc.info

ARRL Affiliated Club	**Mobridge Area Amateur Radio Club**
City:	Mobridge, SD
Section:	SD

ARRL Affiliated Club	**Pierre Amateur Radio Club**
City:	Pierre, SD
Call Sign:	W0PIR
Section:	SD
Links:	www.sdhams.com

ARRL Affiliated Club	**Black Hills Amateur Radio Club**
City:	Rapid City, SD
Call Sign:	W0BLK
Section:	SD
Links:	www.w0blk.org

ARRL Affiliated Club
City:
Call Sign:
Section:
Links:

Sioux Empire Amateur Radio Club
Sioux Falls, SD
W0ZWY
SD
www.w0zwy.org

ARRL Affiliated Club
City:
Call Sign:
Section:
Links:

Deuel County Amateur Radio Club
Volga, SD
WØGC
SD
www.w0gc.org

ARRL Affiliated Club
City:
Call Sign:
Section:
Links:

Lake Area Amateur Radio Klub
Watertown, SD
W0WTN
SD
www.w0wtn.org

APPENDIX B

Amateur Radio License Holders

in

South Dakota
(by City)

FCC Amateur Radio Licenses in Aberdeen

Call Sign: W0DHQ
Arthur F Lanham
916 10th Ave NE
Aberdeen SD 57401

Call Sign: KA0LKS
Judith G Sheldon
1416 10th Ave SE Apt 1
Aberdeen SD 57401

Call Sign: KD0HUK
Timothy L Selzler Jr
1623 10th Ave SW Lot 1218
Aberdeen SD 57401

Call Sign: N0MHZ
John W Emmett Jr
38280 129th St
Aberdeen SD 57401

Call Sign: KA0QVK
Robert L King
821 12th Ave SE
Aberdeen SD 57401

Call Sign: KC0KPQ
Timothy J Kessler
39069 130th St
Aberdeen SD 57401

Call Sign: N9TDE
Marvin L Dreesen
2640 130th St N W 35
Aberdeen SD 57401

Call Sign: WD0FEF
Monte L Bertsch
1617 14th Ave SE
Aberdeen SD 57401

Call Sign: KE5AJO
Elizabeth J Hill

1314 1st Ave S E Apt 204
Aberdeen SD 57401

Call Sign: KD5ZYV
Charles E Hill
1314 1st Ave SE 204
Aberdeen SD 57401

Call Sign: N0ZHU
Merle T Voeller
218 2nd Ave NE
Aberdeen SD 57401

Call Sign: KC0GKC
Chancey S Marshall
523 2nd Ave NE
Aberdeen SD 57401

Call Sign: AA0AH
Kenneth S Mathiason
4911 30th St N
Aberdeen SD 57401

Call Sign: KD0KXV
David A Akers II
13197 382nd Ave
Aberdeen SD 57401

Call Sign: WB0TPF
Arnold C Huizenga
13045 385th Ave
Aberdeen SD 574018447

Call Sign: KB0CUI
Russell D Holtey
13639 387th Ave
Aberdeen SD 574018505

Call Sign: KA0FUW
Randy J Wipf
316 3rd Ave SE
Aberdeen SD 57401

Call Sign: KA0TGA
Paula M Hoerner

711 4th A S W
Aberdeen SD 57401

Call Sign: WD0GQC
Paul E Anderson
906 4th Ave NE
Aberdeen SD 57401

Call Sign: WD0BHX
Anthony P Hoerner
711 4th Ave SW
Aberdeen SD 57401

Call Sign: WD0BHY
Paul M Hoerner
711 4th Ave SW
Aberdeen SD 57401

Call Sign: WD0BHZ
Barbara A Hoerner
711 4th Ave SW
Aberdeen SD 57401

Call Sign: KE0PI
Vivian A Anderson
1205 4th Ave SW
Aberdeen SD 57401

Call Sign: KC7JWB
Doyle D Peterson
316 6th Ave SW 12
Aberdeen SD 57401

Call Sign: KD0JZE
Josh L Halsey
19 7th Ave SE Apt 206
Aberdeen SD 57401

Call Sign: N0OTK
John F Meyer
101 7th Curve
Aberdeen SD 57401

Call Sign: KB0COA
Terry L Bowen

207 8th Ave SE Apt 8
Aberdeen SD 57401

Call Sign: KC0HNU
Gary D Stewart
209 8th Ave SW
Aberdeen SD 57401

Call Sign: WN0W
Dorothy L Gathright
321 9th Ave NE
Aberdeen SD 574012474

Call Sign: KC0NGT
Hub Area Technical School Arc
640 9th Ave SW
Aberdeen SD 57401

Call Sign: W0HUB
Hub Area Technical School Arc
640 9th Ave SW
Aberdeen SD 57401

Call Sign: KC0DHI
Mark B Thompson
1231 Appollo Ave
Aberdeen SD 57401

Call Sign: KC0JKX
Sara N Imberi
1701 E Melgaard Rd 8
Aberdeen SD 57401

Call Sign: KD0HUJ
Tyler G Brown
1886 Eisenhower Cir
Aberdeen SD 57401

Call Sign: KA0KXM
Elaine M Roth
118 Elizabeth Dr
Aberdeen SD 57401

Call Sign: N0BUC
Elmer R Roth

118 Elizabeth Dr
Aberdeen SD 57401

Call Sign: WB0TPC
Paul R Sexton Jr
Jobee Acres
Aberdeen SD 57401

Call Sign: WB0TPH
Peggy Sexton
Jobee Acres
Aberdeen SD 57401

Call Sign: W0BMF
Walter A Brown
1307 Kline N
Aberdeen SD 57401

Call Sign: KC0UTX
Mike D Mikkelson
510 Lincoln St
Aberdeen SD 57401

Call Sign: KA0TVG
Randy G Imberi
1519 Meadowbrooke Ct
Aberdeen SD 574017708

Call Sign: KA0QMM
Lori J Materi
618 N 1st St
Aberdeen SD 57401

Call Sign: KD0MLH
Roby Johnson
1123 N 3rd St
Aberdeen SD 57401

Call Sign: KC0TWP
Mark A Bledsoe
1312 N Arch
Aberdeen SD 57401

Call Sign: KB0OWA
Justin D Shultis

517 N Dakota St
Aberdeen SD 574013047

Call Sign: KB0CUG
Derek A Roberts
1602 N Jackson
Aberdeen SD 57401

Call Sign: KA9OKQ
Charles J Miller
1725 N Jay St
Aberdeen SD 57401

Call Sign: KB9ADY
Teresa C Miller
1725 N Jay St
Aberdeen SD 57401

Call Sign: KB0HAJ
Scott K Mosey
1915 N Jay St
Aberdeen SD 57401

Call Sign: K9QPA
Edward J Wise
1304 N Kline St
Aberdeen SD 57401

Call Sign: N0AHL
Roland L Moerke
1005 N Roosevelt St
Aberdeen SD 57401

Call Sign: W0ZLB
Kenneth B Schutz
817 N State St
Aberdeen SD 57401

Call Sign: KD0OAS
Brandon M Ullrich
1318 N State St
Aberdeen SD 57401

Call Sign: KB0RSC
James R Scarlett

1702 Northview Lane
Aberdeen SD 57401

Call Sign: WB0TPE
Charlotte E Huizenga
3401 NW 30th
Aberdeen SD 57401

Call Sign: WB0TPI
Steve A Blinder
2402 Primrose Ln
Aberdeen SD 574011661

Call Sign: N0GFY
Lavonne M Albrecht
12957 Richmond Heights Dr
Aberdeen SD 57401

Call Sign: KF7GTI
Robert A Bray
719 S 10th St
Aberdeen SD 57401

Call Sign: WD0HWL
Ronald R Bolduan
904 S 10th St
Aberdeen SD 57401

Call Sign: KA0ZEE
Randall W Kingery
411 S 12th St
Aberdeen SD 57401

Call Sign: KA0QVE
Mary S Cross
1721 S 1st St
Aberdeen SD 57401

Call Sign: WD0HWM
George F Cross
1721 S 1st St
Aberdeen SD 574020601

Call Sign: W0GFC
George F Cross

1721 S 1st St
Aberdeen SD 574020601

Call Sign: N0EPX
Doyle L Moffett
506 S 1st St 306
Aberdeen SD 57402

Call Sign: AA0AG
Joan M Mathiason
1209 S 2nd St
Aberdeen SD 57401

Call Sign: W0NWM
Todd A Sayler
1615 S 4th St
Aberdeen SD 57401

Call Sign: K0KLQ
Agnes S Sheldon
1615 S 4th St
Aberdeen SD 574020546

Call Sign: W0NWM
Edwin L Sheldon
1615 S 4th St
Aberdeen SD 574020546

Call Sign: NY0W
Donald A Crampton
1748 S 4th St
Aberdeen SD 57401

Call Sign: KA0GUX
Todd A Sayler
1615 S 4th St
Aberdeen SD 57401

Call Sign: KC0SSE
Jason A Glatt
1322 S 6th St
Aberdeen SD 57401

Call Sign: WB0HJK
Robert H Janssen

1603 S 7th
Aberdeen SD 57401

314 S Boyd
Aberdeen SD 57401

Call Sign: W0KAR
Alan K Mc Farlane
1609 S 7th St
Aberdeen SD 57401

Call Sign: KC0WPA
Ashley R Burdick
1514 S Grant
Aberdeen SD 57401

Call Sign: KC0DHE
Jerry T Taylor
1402 S 8th St
Aberdeen SD 57401

Call Sign: KC0YBZ
Ross D Burdick
1514 S Grant
Aberdeen SD 57401

Call Sign: AC0PF
Jerry T Taylor
1402 S 8th St
Aberdeen SD 57401

Call Sign: KC0WPC
Mercedes A Buchanan
1512 S Grant St
Aberdeen SD 57401

Call Sign: WN0Y
James G Gathright
926 S 9th St
Aberdeen SD 574015801

Call Sign: KC0YDF
Gale R Buchanan
1512 S Grant St
Aberdeen SD 57401

Call Sign: KB0WMP
James L Sjomeling
1004 S 9th St
Aberdeen SD 57401

Call Sign: KC0WPB
Becky L Burdick
1514 S Grant St
Aberdeen SD 57401

Call Sign: KD0GLM
Bob C Brown
401 S 9th St
Aberdeen SD 57401

Call Sign: WA0EZP
Edward L Filegar
1516 S Grant St
Aberdeen SD 57401

Call Sign: KB0GCH
Kristi S Tarnowski
1010 S Aldrich St
Aberdeen SD 57401

Call Sign: KE0YV
Dale R Dauman
18 S Greenwood
Aberdeen SD 57401

Call Sign: KB0GCI
Tommy J Tarnowski
1010 S Aldrich St
Aberdeen SD 57401

Call Sign: KD0PPR
Dean W Johnson
318 S Harrison St
Aberdeen SD 57401

Call Sign: KC0UXZ
Richard L Kezar

Call Sign: N0HST
Michael L Padbury

19 S Harvard
Aberdeen SD 57401

122 S Roosevelt Lot 34
Aberdeen SD 574015023

Call Sign: K0JM
Frank Sonnek
914 S Jay St
Aberdeen SD 57401

Call Sign: W0KLJ
Kenneth L Jones
122 S Roosevelt Lot 34
Aberdeen SD 574015023

Call Sign: WA0WVT
Frank W Sonnek Jr
914 S Jay St
Aberdeen SD 57401

Call Sign: N0NXU
Melissa L Igl
816 S Taft St
Aberdeen SD 57401

Call Sign: WB0ONO
Muriel E Sonnek
914 S Jay St
Aberdeen SD 57401

Call Sign: KA0ZMX
Noel S Johnson
311 S Vivian
Aberdeen SD 57401

Call Sign: KB0ZIT
Nella C Thompson
618 S Kline
Aberdeen SD 57401

Call Sign: WB0STR
James W Downie
103 S Weber
Aberdeen SD 574014846

Call Sign: KB0FWO
Victor W Westerfield
929 S Kline St
Aberdeen SD 57401

Call Sign: WB0JD
James W Downie
103 S Weber
Aberdeen SD 574014846

Call Sign: KD0EUK
Tammy M Merkel
1635 S Melgaard Rd
Aberdeen SD 57401

Call Sign: KO0S
Larry G Roberts
834 S Wells St
Aberdeen SD 57401

Call Sign: KB0TUW
Jamie L Imbery
623 S Park St
Aberdeen SD 57401

Call Sign: KC0DHG
Darin M Hauck
2117 SE Goodrich Ave
Aberdeen SD 57401

Call Sign: W0HOG
Clarence P Wilhelm
621 S Rock St
Aberdeen SD 57402

Call Sign: N0AYK
Gary E Dahlerup
1637 Somerset Dr
Aberdeen SD 57401

Call Sign: KC0LMY
Kenneth L Jones

Call Sign: KG0VQ
Vernon L Zick

904 Squire Ln
Aberdeen SD 57401

Call Sign: WB0VGO
Warren P Blinder
1506 Squire Ln
Aberdeen SD 57401

Call Sign: WA0UWA
Merlin A Schinke
712 SW 4th Ave
Aberdeen SD 57401

Call Sign: K0RMX
Michael J Jacobson
127227 W Bridge Rd
Aberdeen SD 57401

Call Sign: KC0BXX
David L Hintz
2713 W Melgaard Rd
Aberdeen SD 57401

Call Sign: KA0HCW
Ruth M Lamont
Aberdeen SD 57401

Call Sign: KC0KOR
Aaron L Dorn
Aberdeen SD 57402

Call Sign: KC0TGF
Dean L Sinclair
Aberdeen SD 574020592

Call Sign: KD0HQK
Prairie Region Communication
Association
Aberdeen SD 574020611

Call Sign: AB0MW
Prairie Region Communication
Association
Aberdeen SD 574020611

Call Sign: W0ABR
Hub Amateur Radio Club
Aberdeen SD 574020725

Call Sign: WB0VRG
Scott H Blinder
Aberdeen SD 574020955

FCC Amateur Radio Licenses in Alcester

Call Sign: AA0GN
Richard L Grimshaw
30271 478th Ave
Alcester SD 57001

Call Sign: KB0JAD
Martha A Grimshaw
30271 478th Ave
Alcester SD 57001

Call Sign: W0WUU
Melvin C Johnson
307 Circle Dr Apt 1
Alcester SD 57001

Call Sign: AA0TD
Douglas C Stubbs
400 E 1st St
Alcester SD 57001

Call Sign: K5NPR
Nathan P Reiss
505 Jefferson Dr
Alcester SD 57001

Call Sign: KC0RPA
Nathan P Reiss
5050 Jefferson Dr
Alcester SD 57001

Call Sign: KA0NPK
William D Pigman
RR2
Alcester SD 57001

FCC Amateur Radio Licenses in Alexandria

Call Sign: KC0HMQ
Don H Pueppke
42472 251st St
Alexandria SD 57311

Call Sign: KB0VXO
Lynette S Pueppke
42474 251st St
Alexandria SD 57311

Call Sign: AA0YN
Dan S Pueppke
42474 251st St
Alexandria SD 573117612

Call Sign: W0PAK
Radio Amateur Telecommunicators
42474 251st St
Alexandria SD 573117612

Call Sign: KB0PPA
Mark R King
550 9th St
Alexandria SD 57311

Call Sign: KC0CAS
Cindy F King
550 9th St
Alexandria SD 573112211

Call Sign: N0RAN
Noah J Coffer
400 E 4th St
Alexandria SD 57311

FCC Amateur Radio Licenses in Arlington

Call Sign: W0LJB
Wilbert W Simmons
112 1st St S

Arlington SD 57212

Call Sign: KC0TWM
Paula C Fonder
20076 450th Ave
Arlington SD 57212

Call Sign: W0COE
Everett C Dill
113 Park Dr
Arlington SD 57212

Call Sign: KF4RRD
Mike N Glavaris Jr
144 S Point Dr
Arlington SD 57212

Call Sign: KA0SKG
James A Odle
19747 US Hwy 81
Arlington SD 572125503

Call Sign: KC0HWQ
Ian P Odle
19747 US Hwy 81
Arlington SD 572125503

FCC Amateur Radio Licenses in Armour

Call Sign: KA0ZHL
Greg A Farke
39083 284th St
Armour SD 573136500

FCC Amateur Radio Licenses in Artesian

Call Sign: N0XDO
Dennis R Ross
RR2
Artesian SD 57314

Call Sign: KB0BER
Paul L Light

Rt 2
Artesian SD 57314

FCC Amateur Radio Licenses in Astoria

Call Sign: WA0ESJ
Adolph H Andersen
48249 195 St
Astoria SD 57213

FCC Amateur Radio Licenses in Aurora

Call Sign: W0HKG
Bryson R Mc Hardy Sr
Rt 1
Aurora SD 57002

Call Sign: KB0CMX
Terrance A Hill
Rt 1
Aurora SD 57002

Call Sign: KB0ZVF
Julie M Van Dyke
Aurora SD 57002

FCC Amateur Radio Licenses in Avon

Call Sign: WB0SRW
Darwin Dykstra
30763 408th Ave
Avon SD 573155815

FCC Amateur Radio Licenses in Badger

Call Sign: KC0CIA
Donald S Schumacher
Badger SD 57214

FCC Amateur Radio Licenses in Baltic

Call Sign: KB0BBA
David L Hamre
25149 476th Ave
Baltic SD 57003

Call Sign: W0ROE
Martin S Roe
209 Douglas Blvd
Baltic SD 57003

Call Sign: KC8WVW
Nathan S Roe
209 Douglas Blvd
Baltic SD 57003

FCC Amateur Radio Licenses in Batesland

Call Sign: KC0AFR
Eric A Harris
HC 64
Batesland SD 57716

FCC Amateur Radio Licenses in Bath

Call Sign: KC0UCE
Mark R Elsperger
506 5th St Box 552
Bath SD 57427

FCC Amateur Radio Licenses in Belle Fourche

Call Sign: KC0ZQC
Barry H Noor
2034 10th Ave
Belle Fourche SD 57717

Call Sign: K0RXC
Carroll E Cash
2110 11th Ave
Belle Fourche SD 57717

Call Sign: KB0OHO

Ruth A Cash
2110 11th Ave
Belle Fourche SD 57717

Call Sign: N0ORZ
Arthur V Edsall
2058 12th Box 25
Belle Fourche SD 57717

Call Sign: KC0SWS
Dallas Johnson
1612 13th Ave
Belle Fourche SD 57717

Call Sign: KC0BXH
Northern Hills Amateur Radio Club
11050 Bluebell Lane
Belle Fourche SD 57717

Call Sign: KG0GG
Jerry A Hawley
11050 Bluebell Lane
Belle Fourche SD 577177251

Call Sign: WD0EUK
Linda S Hawley
11050 Bluebell Lane
Belle Fourche SD 577177251

Call Sign: KC0SWR
Christopher A Raber
111 Custer St Lot 409
Belle Fourche SD 57717

Call Sign: KC0ULZ
Bruce A Jennings
19248 Iron Horse Cir
Belle Fourche SD 57717

Call Sign: N0QWW
Melissa M Mitchell
RR2
Belle Fourche SD 57717

Call Sign: W0LZZ

Carl E Smith
1832 S Mill St
Belle Fourche SD 57717

Call Sign: KD0QCG
Richard T Banks II
Statesboro Dr
Belle Fourche SD 57717

Call Sign: KC0IOX
Eric W Stover
Statesboro Dr
Belle Fourche SD 57717

Call Sign: KD0AYO
Deron Kazmier
15851 US Hwy 85
Belle Fourche SD 57717

Call Sign: N0NBB
Laura R Edsall
Belle Fourche SD 57717

Call Sign: AB0GH
John J Whitney
Belle Fourche SD 577170039

Call Sign: KB0YAM
Bruce B Brown
Belle Fourche SD 577170039

FCC Amateur Radio Licenses in Beresford

Call Sign: KB0ZEK
Jerry L Beggs
400 E Maple 11
Beresford SD 57004

Call Sign: KC2AKU
Christopher F Halm
205 N 8th St
Beresford SD 57004

Call Sign: KC0RPB

Tony W Akland
311 S 1st
Beresford SD 57004

FCC Amateur Radio Licenses in Big Stone City

Call Sign: W0WLB
Donald V Mc Farland
610 3rd Ave
Big Stone City SD 57216

Call Sign: KA0ASC
Steve L Rabe
101 High St
Big Stone City SD 57216

Call Sign: KC0CGR
Robert G Goergen
105 High St
Big Stone City SD 57216

Call Sign: KC0DPD
Teresa M Goergen
105 High St
Big Stone City SD 57216

Call Sign: KC0CYN
Gregory G Hooser
302 High St
Big Stone City SD 57216

Call Sign: N0BDV
Ivan T Thomson
803 Mitchell Ave
Big Stone City SD 57216

Call Sign: KE0RK
Ronald C Heffron
48445 US Hwy 12
Big Stone City SD 57216

FCC Amateur Radio Licenses in Bison

Call Sign: WB0DWH
Albert Hoff
12785 168th Ave
Bison SD 57620

Call Sign: KC0GPK
Samuel R Drown
Bison SD 576200232

FCC Amateur Radio Licenses in Black Hawk

Call Sign: N0TYN
Jeffrey C Woods
6417 Cottonwood Ct
Black Hawk SD 57718

Call Sign: KB0PMZ
Christine A Bump
7101 Diann Dr
Black Hawk SD 57718

Call Sign: KD0FRG
William C Steele
4266 Fleetwood Dr
Black Hawk SD 57718

Call Sign: KB0LDK
Dean A Hatch
8251 Foothills Rd
Black Hawk SD 57718

Call Sign: KC0KFW
Paul J Molnar
7401 Hellen Dr
Black Hawk SD 57718

Call Sign: KF0CS
Stefan Steger
10004 High Meadows Dr
Black Hawk SD 57718

Call Sign: WA6MNC
Gerald T Scharer
6940 Leisure Ln

Black Hawk SD 57718

Call Sign: KC0KT
Richard P Renka
11400 Lofty Pines Rd
Black Hawk SD 57718

Call Sign: W0COV
Richard C Smith
6813 Logan
Black Hawk SD 57718

Call Sign: KC0IBU
Tamaria N Smith
6813 Logan Dr
Black Hawk SD 57718

Call Sign: N0HUL
Richard B Hexem
5150 Merritt Rd
Black Hawk SD 57718

Call Sign: W7RMC
Gene V Snyder
6830 Mulberry Dr
Black Hawk SD 577189897

Call Sign: WB0VCB
Theodore B Pukas
10805 N High Meadows Dr
Black Hawk SD 57718

Call Sign: W0JCE
James A Rundell
10000 Romel Dr
Black Hawk SD 57718

Call Sign: KC0VDD
Bruce G Conlee
10301 Romel Dr
Black Hawk SD 577188644

Call Sign: KC0VDK
Bruce G Conlee
10301 Romel Dr

Black Hawk SD 577188644

Call Sign: K0NLE
Bruce G Conlee
10301 Romel Dr
Black Hawk SD 577188644

Call Sign: KB0DLB
Robert C Strand
7907 Timberline Rd
Black Hawk SD 57718

Call Sign: KB0HXW
Darlene M Michel
9702 Walden Ln
Black Hawk SD 57718

Call Sign: KB0ZNE
Billy L Hilton
7705 Woodland Dr
Black Hawk SD 57718

Call Sign: K0BLH
Billy L Hilton
7705 Woodland Dr
Black Hawk SD 57718

FCC Amateur Radio Licenses in Box Elder

Call Sign: W7AXB
Herman A Hageman Jr
514 Americas Way
Box Elder SD 577197600

Call Sign: KC7DRC
Philip R Edwards
514 Americas Way 1054
Box Elder SD 577197600

Call Sign: KG6SIS
Gregory G Pyros
514 Americas Way 1256
Box Elder SD 577197600

Call Sign: KD0KYK
Duane A Grooms
514 Americas Way 1301
Box Elder SD 577191301

Call Sign: KB6VOW
Ardelle M Coult
514 Americas Way 1541
Box Elder SD 577197600

Call Sign: WA6AAL
Roger A Coult
514 Americas Way 1541
Box Elder SD 577197600

Call Sign: KD5DIV
David H Zittel
514 Americas Way 1548
Box Elder SD 57719

Call Sign: K7YJ
Minor W Cross
514 Americas Way 1871
Box Elder SD 577197600

Call Sign: WZ7S
Judith A Cross
514 Americas Way 1871
Box Elder SD 577197600

Call Sign: KD0PYT
Robert D Swanson
514 Americas Way 2016
Box Elder SD 57719

Call Sign: KD0PYS
Sandra A Swanson
514 Americas Way 2016
Box Elder SD 57719

Call Sign: KF1S
David L Lippke
514 Americas Way 2248
Box Elder SD 57719

Call Sign: KB6HI
Harvey R Girard
514 Americas Way 2355
Box Elder SD 577197600

Call Sign: K5TT
James M Hood
514 Americas Way 2490
Box Elder SD 57719

Call Sign: N9LBJ
George W Loutzenhiser
514 Americas Way 2532
Box Elder SD 577197600

Call Sign: N9LVL
Linda L Loutzenhiser
514 Americas Way 2532
Box Elder SD 577197600

Call Sign: KD0JXR
Jay O Casey
514 Americas Way 2572
Box Elder SD 577197600

Call Sign: KB9EIB
Rebekah C Detamore
514 Americas Way 2742
Box Elder SD 577197600

Call Sign: WB9NYR
William R Detamore
514 Americas Way 2742
Box Elder SD 577197600

Call Sign: WA2IAC
Gregg W Squires
514 Americas Way 2762
Box Elder SD 577197600

Call Sign: KU9L
David M Knapp
514 Americas Way 2982
Box Elder SD 577197600

Call Sign: KB9YYI
Sheila J Knapp
514 Americas Way 2982
Box Elder SD 577197600

Call Sign: K9PM
Paul M Mueller
514 Americas Way 3095
Box Elder SD 57719

Call Sign: KI6IRP
Stanley K Foster
514 Americas Way 3321
Box Elder SD 57719

Call Sign: AC0WN
Julie A Mcgrew
514 Americas Way 3407
Box Elder SD 577197600

Call Sign: KD0OVR
Randolph W Mcgrew
514 Americas Way 3407
Box Elder SD 577197600

Call Sign: K5VU
Jeffrey D Sykes
514 Americas Way 3472
Box Elder SD 577197600

Call Sign: K3AL
Duane M Reese
514 Americas Way 3579
Box Elder SD 57719

Call Sign: K6KDK
Daniel G Hyman
514 Americas Way 3610
Box Elder SD 57719

Call Sign: KM6HK
Daniel G Hyman
514 Americas Way 3610
Box Elder SD 57719

Call Sign: WS9F
Matthew D Finlayson
514 Americas Way 3813
Box Elder SD 577197600

Call Sign: N3QXR
Thomas F Hodill
514 Americas Way Apt 3151
Box Elder SD 57719

Call Sign: KD0IVB
Emily A Snavely
523 Falcon Dr
Box Elder SD 57719

Call Sign: KC0RTW
Lew M Mcdowell
701 Harmony Rd
Box Elder SD 57719

Call Sign: KE7DEX
Julie R Key
240 N Ellsworth Rd 114
Box Elder SD 57719

Call Sign: K0MDK
Michael D Key
240 N Ellsworth Rd Lot 114
Box Elder SD 57719

Call Sign: NR5A
Jerry E Felts
508 Prairie Rd
Box Elder SD 57719

Call Sign: KA0PCB
Joseph M Johengen
Box Elder SD 577190417

FCC Amateur Radio Licenses in Brandon

Call Sign: KB0JLV
Ernest L Janssen
48250 264th St

Brandon SD 57005

Call Sign: WA0CWX
Donna Y Albers
48261 268th St
Brandon SD 57005

Call Sign: KD0HRP
Wayne W Miss
313 8th Ave
Brandon SD 57005

Call Sign: KB0APE
Gregory G Anderson
26663 Brownstone Ave
Brandon SD 57005

Call Sign: W0GUS
Gregory G Anderson
26663 Brownstone Ave
Brandon SD 57005

Call Sign: N0YZY
Eugene D Bennett
1400 E Custer Pky
Brandon SD 57005

Call Sign: KD0LRU
David R Barnes
217 E Glenwood
Brandon SD 57005

Call Sign: WB0MQA
David R Barnes
217 E Glenwood
Brandon SD 57005

Call Sign: KC0WNF
Ryan P Greene
209 E Maria Lane
Brandon SD 57005

Call Sign: WA0YFR
John F Hertz
200 E Vera Ln

Brandon SD 57005

Call Sign: K4OUT
James V Irby III
905 Maywood St
Brandon SD 57005

Call Sign: WB4QYX
Sharon C Irby
905 Maywood St
Brandon SD 57005

Call Sign: N0DCN
Francis V Larson
26255 Mc Hardy Rd
Brandon SD 57005

Call Sign: KD0EUA
Daniel J Christensen
517 Meadowlark Court
Brandon SD 57005

Call Sign: KC0ION
Peter R Schilf
2801 N Oak Rd
Brandon SD 57005

Call Sign: KB0SJK
William H Leshovsky
517 N Yellowstone
Brandon SD 57005

Call Sign: WU0L
Mark L Meyer
504 Riverwood Cir
Brandon SD 57005

Call Sign: N0PTX
Wayne D Kerslake
RR1
Brandon SD 57005

Call Sign: KD0IIU
Charles R Henson
309 S 3rd Ave

Brandon SD 57005

Call Sign: K0WXP
Shawn B Pope
717 S 6th Ave
Brandon SD 57005

Call Sign: K0FKJ
Raymond J Christensen
112 S Needles Dr
Brandon SD 57005

Call Sign: WA0YRI
Alfred Belk
106 S Sandstone Ave Apt 7
Brandon SD 57005

Call Sign: KC0EOM
Ryan M Chase
416 S Yellowstone Dr
Brandon SD 57005

Call Sign: N0YGT
Thomas A Bodoh
301 Sunset Dr
Brandon SD 57005

Call Sign: KB0VMM
Molly A Moor
613 Switch Grass Trail
Brandon SD 57005

Call Sign: KD0JYE
Wyatt J Walton
1115 Teakwood St 2
Brandon SD 57005

FCC Amateur Radio Licenses in Bridgewater

Call Sign: KC7YUR
Evelyn J Hofer
630 E 2nd St
Bridgewater SD 573192100

Call Sign: K7GCO
Kenneth W Glanzer
43261 Hwy 42
Bridgewater SD 57319

Call Sign: W0LMB
South Dakota Antenna Club
43261 Hwy 42
Bridgewater SD 57319

FCC Amateur Radio Licenses in Bristol

Call Sign: W0QGZ
Ellis M Day
417 3rd St E
Bristol SD 57219

FCC Amateur Radio Licenses in Britton

Call Sign: N0CFS
Fred B Eikamp
1201 3rd St
Britton SD 57430

Call Sign: KA0ACO
Lloyd P Duerre
105 9th Ave
Britton SD 57430

Call Sign: KB0NZC
Wendell W Lewis
Britton SD 57430

FCC Amateur Radio Licenses in Brookings

Call Sign: KB0NOC
Michael J Palm
204 10th St W
Brookings SD 57006

Call Sign: WA0OML
George H Duffey

628 11th Ave
Brookings SD 570061526

Call Sign: KC0GIX
Richard A Haub
123 12th Ave S 1
Brookings SD 57006

Call Sign: KD0BHE
Laurence M Coderre
901 15th St E 1006
Brookings SD 57006

Call Sign: KA0SNH
Arlen E Rosvold
518 17th Ave S
Brookings SD 57006

Call Sign: KB0CHJ
Trudi Mofle
1202 17th Ave S
Brookings SD 57006

Call Sign: KB0AUQ
David B Larson
2126 17th Ave S
Brookings SD 57006

Call Sign: KB0ZW
Gary B Peterson
512 20th Ave
Brookings SD 57006

Call Sign: KB5ZOM
Paul K Smith
2110 22 Ave S Lot 6
Brookings SD 57006

Call Sign: KG0XM
David M Wiesner
508 2nd Ave
Brookings SD 57006

Call Sign: KC0FXS
Robert W Blackketter

719 2nd St
Brookings SD 57006

Call Sign: N0CFW
Edwin J Luetzow
2325 32nd Ave
Brookings SD 57006

Call Sign: W0BXO
Radio Research Club
307 3rd Ave
Brookings SD 57006

Call Sign: KB0NLZ
Charles R Engelmann
20601 470th Ave
Brookings SD 57006

Call Sign: K0PH
Jerry E Cooley
202 4th St
Brookings SD 57006

Call Sign: WB0QDO
Donald D De Greef
102 58th Ave S
Brookings SD 57006

Call Sign: KC0GGO
Eva M Degreef
102 58th Ave S
Brookings SD 570066518

Call Sign: KA0SGH
James L Anderson
611 6th Ave
Brookings SD 57006

Call Sign: K0DEL
Edward C Collins
905 6th Ave
Brookings SD 57006

Call Sign: KB0HCB
Timothy B Nielsen

902 6th St
Brookings SD 57006

1627 Buffalo Trail
Brookings SD 57006

Call Sign: KA0AXG
Donald A Aulner
722 7th Ave
Brookings SD 57006

Call Sign: K0GCT
Gene R Eidsness
808 Christine Ave 102
Brookings SD 57006

Call Sign: W0KXZ
John W Headley
816 7th Ave
Brookings SD 570061308

Call Sign: KB0RQF
Raymond W Ofstedal
1044 Circle Dr
Brookings SD 57006

Call Sign: WA0JH
John W Headley
816 7th Ave
Brookings SD 570061308

Call Sign: K0AZD
Wilbur V Kraft
1715 Dakota St
Brookings SD 570062346

Call Sign: N0OQI
Matt R Johnson
534 7th Ave S 6
Brookings SD 57006

Call Sign: WB0LUI
Sidney A Johnson
1821 Derdall Dr
Brookings SD 57006

Call Sign: N0XDQ
Todd L Struwe
229 8th St W
Brookings SD 57006

Call Sign: KB0FTV
Barbara A Johnson
1807 Eberlein Dr
Brookings SD 57006

Call Sign: KB0NLX
Kathy J Struwe
130 9th St
Brookings SD 57006

Call Sign: WD0FET
Perry R Johnson
1807 Eberlein Dr
Brookings SD 57006

Call Sign: KI0FN
James E Hanson
3334 Aspen Ave
Brookings SD 57006

Call Sign: KC0FLM
Lawrence L Peterson
2038 Elmwood Dr
Brookings SD 57006

Call Sign: KB0PYF
Angela D Floro
157 Brown Box 2801
Brookings SD 570071996

Call Sign: KF0SP
Richard A Sandvold
214 Flint Pass
Brookings SD 57006

Call Sign: WB0YAS
Gerald A Friezen

Call Sign: KB0ZWU
Ken C Laturnus

Gilley
Brookings SD 57006

Call Sign: KB0QEF
Richard O Canaday
212 Half Moon Rd
Brookings SD 57006

Call Sign: KB0NOD
Barbara J Palm
509 Hunters Ridge Rd
Brookings SD 57006

Call Sign: WB0CPW
Darel J Palm
509 Hunters Ridge Rd
Brookings SD 57006

Call Sign: KC0TWN
David C Peterson
2026 Kansas Dr
Brookings SD 57006

Call Sign: N0KGR
Kenneth G Robinson Jr
1428 King Arthur Court
Brookings SD 57006

Call Sign: N0JHO
Robert A Meyer
1706 Lincoln Ln
Brookings SD 57006

Call Sign: KA0WEH
Dale L West
1919 Lincoln Ln
Brookings SD 57006

Call Sign: N0OJJ
Joseph C Portz
1009 Main Ave S
Brookings SD 57006

Call Sign: N0PUA
Robert W Sachen

1802 Main Ave S
Brookings SD 57006

Call Sign: N0XDS
Dean B Christie
2432 Main Ave S
Brookings SD 57006

Call Sign: W0FFP
Russell C Nielsen
410 Medary S 30
Brookings SD 57006

Call Sign: KC0FPB
Clinton F Groves
1035 N Main Apt A 3
Brookings SD 57006

Call Sign: KC0FLL
Harold L Manson
1047 N Main Ave 9A
Brookings SD 57006

Call Sign: KC0ZHE
Arthur A Wilber
411 Ohio Dr
Brookings SD 57006

Call Sign: KB0VSY
Gloria J Lokkeberg
913 Onaka Trail
Brookings SD 57006

Call Sign: W0KQO
Arnold L Smith
636 Park Ave
Brookings SD 57006

Call Sign: W0UDI
Robert T Bates
839 Park Ave Apt 2
Brookings SD 57006

Call Sign: KB0EG
Allan R Jones

1516 Pine Ridge Rd
Brookings SD 57006

Call Sign: KB0CHP
Jan V Hayden Pearson
RR2
Brookings SD 57006

Call Sign: KC0ONK
Kenneth G Robinson Jr
410 S Medary Ave Lot 1
Brookings SD 57006

Call Sign: N0NKR
Kenneth G Robinson Jr
410 S Medary Ave Lot 1
Brookings SD 57006

Call Sign: KA0SLD
Randy L Van Dyke
1800 Santee Pass
Brookings SD 57006

Call Sign: KB0BID
Vicki R Larson
1132 Squire Ct
Brookings SD 57006

Call Sign: WB0TSR
David A Larson
1132 Squire Ct
Brookings SD 570063966

Call Sign: KB9CDT
Michael A Moxon
4030 US Hghway 14
Brookings SD 57006

Call Sign: KB9CRC
Steven R Moxon
4030 US Hwy 14
Brookings SD 570066530

Call Sign: KA0SPW
Christopher H Nichols

1209 Windsor Dr
Brookings SD 57006

Call Sign: WA0JLH
Lloyd W Haase
2322 Yorkshire Dr 107
Brookings SD 57006

Call Sign: N0IME
Alan S Lundy
Brookings SD 57006

Call Sign: KD0MER
Daniel T Klosterman
Brookings SD 57006

Call Sign: KD0MET
Ezekiel M Klosterman
Brookings SD 57006

Call Sign: KD0MES
Joshua L Klosterman
Brookings SD 57006

FCC Amateur Radio Licenses in Bruce

Call Sign: KC0FLK
Harlan G Feldhus
406 1st St Bx394
Bruce SD 57220

Call Sign: KA0AYV
Roger M Bommersbach
20334 460th Ave
Bruce SD 57220

Call Sign: KB0CEO
Jonathon M Moir
Bruce SD 57220

FCC Amateur Radio Licenses in Buffalo

Call Sign: WA0CUL

Frank R Clark
73 4th St
Buffalo SD 57720

Call Sign: WB0ZMW
Norman N Westers
Buffalo SD 57720

FCC Amateur Radio Licenses in Burbank

Call Sign: KC0WKI
Douglas A Langley
31651 471st Ave
Burbank SD 57010

Call Sign: KB0CF
Richard D Cayce
46896 Main St
Burbank SD 57010

Call Sign: WD0DBX
Vincent A Kub
RR1
Burbank SD 57010

Call Sign: WB0WZZ
Randy S Rumelhart
32032 White St
Burbank SD 570100015

Call Sign: WQ0W
Joseph T Night
32023 White St
Burbank SD 57010

Call Sign: NE0G
Delbert D Rumelhart
Burbank SD 57010

Call Sign: WB0WZY
Lila J Rumelhart
Burbank SD 57010

FCC Amateur Radio Licenses in Canistota

Call Sign: N0IQF
Richard L Osborne
Canistota SD 57012

Call Sign: KA0CLH
Robert E Moeckel
Canistota SD 570120126

Call Sign: N0WWQ
Le Nora A Moeckel
Canistota SD 570120126

FCC Amateur Radio Licenses in Canton

Call Sign: KC0DRO
David A Ackerman
47799 279th St
Canton SD 57013

Call Sign: KB0VFR
Canton Middle School Communications
In Area
47785 281st St
Canton SD 57013

Call Sign: KA0HVX
David W Mathison
48172 285th St
Canton SD 57013

Call Sign: KC0EAP
Jeremy D Ackerman
47799 297th St
Canton SD 57103

Call Sign: KB0FWA
Sandra J Ostraat
27780 482nd Ave
Canton SD 57013

Call Sign: N0LTR

John E Ostraat
27780 482nd Ave
Canton SD 57013

Call Sign: WB0CKN
Richard A Jaqua
27546 483rd Ave
Canton SD 570135511

Call Sign: KC0RXA
Brandon G Bergren
410 E 2nd St
Canton SD 57013

Call Sign: W0ZLS
Robert W Wissink
505 E 4th 1
Canton SD 57013

Call Sign: KB0HOF
Tracy L Montgomery
404 E 4th St Apt 1
Canton SD 57013

Call Sign: KB7UP
Kenneth R Cressman
503 N Bartlett St
Canton SD 57013

Call Sign: N0KMK
Reynold C Eneboe
418 N Broadway
Canton SD 57013

Call Sign: KB0KEG
Luke J Albers
708 N Lincoln
Canton SD 57013

Call Sign: NN0R
William A Slade
617 N Milwaukee St
Canton SD 57013

Call Sign: KE0HP

Donna E M Kappenman
52 N Park Ln
Canton SD 57013

Call Sign: N0GX
Kevin C Kappenman
52 N Park Ln
Canton SD 57013

Call Sign: N0OXS
Charles J Kappenman
52 N Park Ln
Canton SD 57013

Call Sign: K0SZM
Larry L Minor
9 Park Ln
Canton SD 57013

Call Sign: KB0NYW
Emily S Nadaud
RR1
Canton SD 57013

Call Sign: KC0UYS
Anthony C Lund
27726 SD Hwy 11
Canton SD 57013

Call Sign: N0RFS
Clement S Tucker
308 W 12th St
Canton SD 57013

Call Sign: N6NZK
Bruce A Wichers
408 W 12th St
Canton SD 57013

Call Sign: N0STT
Edward F Stowell
613 W 3rd St
Canton SD 57013

Call Sign: N0IMV

David L Skaien
420 W 6th
Canton SD 57013

Call Sign: KB0HOG
Sharon R Skaien
420 W 6th St
Canton SD 57013

Call Sign: KC0BHP
Jeffrey A Hoogeterp
711 W 7th St
Canton SD 57013

Call Sign: KC0BHO
Harlan L Hoogeterp
711 W 7th St
Canton SD 57013

FCC Amateur Radio Licenses in Caputa

Call Sign: KC0VZN
Casey J Tippmann
15560 233rd
Caputa SD 57725

FCC Amateur Radio Licenses in Castlewood

Call Sign: KD0HWM
Lynn M Olson
46002 184th St
Castlewood SD 57223

Call Sign: KB0VXD
Charles K Olson
46002 184th St
Castlewood SD 57223

Call Sign: KD0RHR
Rylan M Ojala
703 2nd Ave N 2
Castlewood SD 57223

Call Sign: WB0WON
Bonnie M Koppman
18239 459th Ave
Castlewood SD 57223

Call Sign: WA0UHH
Edwin E Davis
Box 141
Castlewood SD 57223

Call Sign: KB0IUO
Lloyd C Stavick
RR2
Castlewood SD 57223

Call Sign: N0MEA
John E Griffith
211 S 3rd Ave Box 20
Castlewood SD 57223

Call Sign: KB0KBJ
Tauno S Olson
Castlewood SD 57223

FCC Amateur Radio Licenses in Centerville

Call Sign: K0GDS
Delmer L Hybertson
46110 288th St
Centerville SD 57014

Call Sign: WB0YOA
Wayne H Wessels
431 Iowa St
Centerville SD 570140384

Call Sign: W0LXD
Stanford D Schmiedt
410 Lincoln
Centerville SD 57014

Call Sign: N7VWV
Laura J Ostrem
401 Main St

Centerville SD 57014

Call Sign: W7CW
Jay E Ostrem
401 Main St
Centerville SD 57014

Call Sign: W0SCT
Lester R Lauritzen
Rt 2
Centerville SD 57014

FCC Amateur Radio Licenses in Chamberlain

Call Sign: W0TNU
Lawrence W Bergner
25761 344th Ave
Chamberlain SD 573256704

Call Sign: KA0QNR
James C Leiferman
200 E Stearns
Chamberlain SD 57325

Call Sign: W0CMJ
Earl H Biskeborn
RR1
Chamberlain SD 57325

Call Sign: WB0HUY
Mark B Wagner
Chamberlain SD 57325

Call Sign: N0WHK
Forrest E Norton
Chamberlain SD 57325

Call Sign: KA9NYN
David R Mohr
Chamberlain SD 573250282

FCC Amateur Radio Licenses in Chancellor

Call Sign: W0EKT
Alan H Schneiderman
Chancellor SD 57015

FCC Amateur Radio Licenses in Chester

Call Sign: W0SIR
Richard L Neish
5231 Southshore Dr
Chester SD 570160100

FCC Amateur Radio Licenses in Claire City

Call Sign: WD0BMR
Katherine A Balvin
10825 452nd Ave
Claire City SD 57224

Call Sign: WD0BMS
David E Balvin
10825 452nd Ave
Claire City SD 57224

Call Sign: KA0UMY
David O Balvin
Rt 1
Claire City SD 57224

Call Sign: KA0UMZ
Edward C Balvin
Rt 1
Claire City SD 57224

Call Sign: N0RXL
Evelyn M Vasend
Rt 1
Claire City SD 57224

Call Sign: WA0CGB
Rubin G Vasend
Rt 1
Claire City SD 57224

FCC Amateur Radio Licenses in Clark

Call Sign: N0MJN
Kendal A Heiden
42626 164th St
Clark SD 57225

Call Sign: AB0H
Michael E Seefeldt
42645 180th St
Clark SD 57225

Call Sign: WA6AUU
Robert H Hubbard
507 N Smith
Clark SD 572251250

Call Sign: K0ZEY
Donald E Nelson
RR1
Clark SD 57225

FCC Amateur Radio Licenses in Clear Lake

Call Sign: KG0TI
Steven L Bohlen
47566 184th St
Clear Lake SD 57226

Call Sign: N0TAW
Robert J Schmidt
607 3rd St W
Clear Lake SD 57226

Call Sign: N0YAE
Breck A Hamann
18280 480th Ave
Clear Lake SD 57226

Call Sign: KA0RAC
Terry L Kelly
711 4th St W
Clear Lake SD 57226

Call Sign: KD0JSJ
Duane L Martin
17945 S Hwy 15
Clear Lake SD 57226

Call Sign: KK0KK
Duane L Martin
17945 S Hwy 15
Clear Lake SD 57226

Call Sign: KC0TFD
Deuel County Amateur Radio Club
Clear Lake SD 57226

Call Sign: W0GC
Deuel County Amateur Radio Club
Clear Lake SD 57226

Call Sign: KA7LCC
Elaine C Riggle
Clear Lake SD 57226

Call Sign: N7CTY
Robert D Riggle
Clear Lake SD 57226

Call Sign: WA0YIN
Danny W Kelly
Clear Lake SD 57226

Call Sign: KC0KWA
Kirk P Berge
Clear Lake SD 57226

Call Sign: KC0TWL
Blaine A Franken
Clear Lake SD 57226

Call Sign: KC0TWK
Mark R Law
Clear Lake SD 572260487

FCC Amateur Radio Licenses in Colman

Call Sign: KC0AM
John S Walker
22471 470th Ave
Colman SD 570177127

Call Sign: KB7QBP
Terry L Mc Kenzie
23503 472nd Ave
Colman SD 57017

Call Sign: AB0XI
Terry L Mc Kenzie
23503 472nd Ave
Colman SD 57017

Call Sign: WA0TXG
Henry G Kohlmeyer
Rt 3
Colman SD 57017

Call Sign: KA0DEZ
John D Lellelid
224 S Loban St
Colman SD 570170232

Call Sign: KC0NQM
Ella J Lellelid
224 S Loban St
Colman SD 570170232

Call Sign: N0HIN
Harold Benedict
Colman SD 57017

FCC Amateur Radio Licenses in Colome

Call Sign: KC0WMY
Wayne B Piper
31567 284th St
Colome SD 57528

Call Sign: WA0TNM
James M Nance

32270 285th St
Colome SD 57528

Call Sign: W0WE
Chandlor E Shippy
29375 324th Ave
Colome SD 575286017

Call Sign: AB0OB
William J Schreiner
Colome SD 57528

FCC Amateur Radio Licenses in Colton

Call Sign: KC0RWV
Steve D Wolterstorff
24863 468th Ave
Colton SD 57018

Call Sign: W0SDW
Steve D Wolterstorff
24863 468th Ave
Colton SD 57018

Call Sign: KB0ROT
Kenneth J Carlson
606 E 4th St
Colton SD 57018

Call Sign: KB5YQH
Robert M Butts
104 S Main Ave
Colton SD 57018

Call Sign: N0KRX
Bruce L Overgard
109 W 4th
Colton SD 57018

FCC Amateur Radio Licenses in Corsica

Call Sign: K0UXC
Delmar G Markus

26899 383rd Ave
Corsica SD 573285127

Call Sign: WD0BJZ
Evan L Baas
RR1
Corsica SD 57328

FCC Amateur Radio Licenses in Cresbard

Call Sign: WB0SSC
Daniel G Sheldon
Cresbard SD 57435

FCC Amateur Radio Licenses in Crooks

Call Sign: KD0QMM
Don S Wipf
25702 471st Ave
Crooks SD 57020

FCC Amateur Radio Licenses in Custer

Call Sign: KD0GRG
Robert D Kampfer
25564 Carroll Creek Rd
Custer SD 57730

Call Sign: KF0VT
Edwin L Brady
420 Crook St
Custer SD 57730

Call Sign: KB0TH
Dan N Stearns
HCR 83
Custer SD 57730

Call Sign: K0DPD
James R Winter
HCR 83
Custer SD 57730

Call Sign: KD0GED
Harry J Rodoni
25458 Lassiter Ct
Custer SD 57730

Call Sign: WB0OQE
Bill S Amundson
4 Lincoln St
Custer SD 57730

Call Sign: KD3RZ
David A Frankenbery
230 N 11th St
Custer SD 57730

Call Sign: W0YMU
Rolland A Fried
Rt 1
Custer SD 57730

Call Sign: WA0NZA
Lyndell S Smith
Rt 1
Custer SD 57730

Call Sign: KB0JAA
John L Miller
Rt 1
Custer SD 57330

Call Sign: W0DDT
Leslie A Johnson
Rt 1
Custer SD 57730

Call Sign: WN6QJN
Peter R Burkett
25422 Sidney Park Rd
Custer SD 57730

Call Sign: KC0QJW
Mark A Mills
24853 Wild Turkey Dr
Custer SD 577307139

Call Sign: WA6JRY
Morris S Burch
12059 Woodford Rd
Custer SD 57730

Call Sign: N6ATH
Paul D Le Clair
Custer SD 577303058

Call Sign: KB0QDG
Brian J Hartmann
Custer SD 57730

Call Sign: WD0DDT
Leslie A Johnson
Custer SD 57730

Call Sign: KD0DZK
Carl G Gola
Custer SD 57730

Call Sign: W0BLC
Carl G Gola
Custer SD 57730

Call Sign: KD0JXS
Robert L Drury
Custer SD 57730

Call Sign: W0JAC
Jack M Botsford
Custer SD 577300889

FCC Amateur Radio Licenses in Dakota Dunes

Call Sign: K2KBL
George E Clark
443 S Royal Troon Cir
Dakota Dunes SD 57049

Call Sign: KA0PHA
Paul E Johnson
309 W Pinehurst Trail

Dakota Dunes SD 57049

Call Sign: KC0QCX
Todd M Lacroix
401 W Pineurst Trl
Dakota Dunes SD 57049

FCC Amateur Radio Licenses in Dallas

Call Sign: KC0NSA
Treg R Gruhn
33198 287th St
Dallas SD 57529

Call Sign: KA0SWL
Elmer D Whitepipe
RR3
Dallas SD 57529

Call Sign: N9FZW
Michael L De Amann
Rr5
Dallas SD 57529

FCC Amateur Radio Licenses in Deadwood

Call Sign: KD0KMX
Mary C Deck
12162 High Pines Rd
Deadwood SD 577327346

Call Sign: W0PYZ
Gene H Deck
12162 High Pines Rd
Deadwood SD 577327346

Call Sign: KD0MPN
Edward C Nelson
31 Mile High Dr
Deadwood SD 57732

Call Sign: WA0WNF
Edward C Nelson

31 Mile High Dr
Deadwood SD 57732

Call Sign: KD0GM
Alan J Hicks
38 Washington St
Deadwood SD 57732

Call Sign: N0ERL
Darleen A Hicks
38 Washington St
Deadwood SD 57732

Call Sign: K0INJ
Howard A Muchow
Deadwood SD 57732

Call Sign: K0QCX
Elvin D Long
Deadwood SD 57732

Call Sign: W1GV
Stanley P Gibilisco
Deadwood SD 57732

Call Sign: KD0IDU
Deborah Mills
Deadwood SD 57732

Call Sign: KD0IDT
Dennis M Mills
Deadwood SD 57732

Call Sign: N7MOG
William A Collister
Deadwood SD 577320146

FCC Amateur Radio Licenses in Dell Rapids

Call Sign: KC0PMC
Loren Maserek
E 4th St Apt 2
Dell Rapids SD 57022

Call Sign: WB0USF
Jerry Wagner
1113 Harrison Ave
Dell Rapids SD 570221109

Call Sign: KD0HJB
Jonathon Hansen
320 W 9th St
Dell Rapids SD 57022

Call Sign: KB0WJN
Evelyn J Huntimer
509 W 9th St
Dell Rapids SD 57022

Call Sign: KI0CW
William P Huntimer
509 W 9th St
Dell Rapids SD 57022

Call Sign: K4JOB
John O Barnett
602 W 9th St
Dell Rapids SD 57022

Call Sign: N0OT
John O Barnett
602 W 9th St
Dell Rapids SD 57022

Call Sign: K0ASW
Craig E Kumerfield
Dell Rapids SD 57022

FCC Amateur Radio Licenses in DeSmet

Call Sign: WB0CHM
Dennis L Helder
43148 197 St
DeSmet SD 57231

Call Sign: KB0VTR
Karen Brown
208 3rd St

DeSmet SD 57231

Call Sign: W0VTX
Donna M Stewart
208 3rd St SE
Desmet SD 57231

FCC Amateur Radio Licenses in Dimock

Call Sign: WB0ZZI
Carl R Struck
Dimock SD 57331

FCC Amateur Radio Licenses in Eagle Butte

Call Sign: W0KUX
Walter A Woods
646 N Heart
Eagle Butte SD 57625

Call Sign: KC0BBI
Leon M Veaux
Eagle Butte SD 57625

Call Sign: WD0FIM
Joe Burckhard
Eagle Butte SD 57625

FCC Amateur Radio Licenses in Edgemont

Call Sign: K0AIE
Albert H Gull
110 4th Ave
Edgemont SD 57735

Call Sign: WA0MRZ
Elmer C Olmstead
407 4th Ave
Edgemont SD 57735

Call Sign: AA0LD
James D Wolfe

Edgemont SD 57735

Call Sign: W0ZUS
Duane L Angerhofer
Edgemont SD 57735

FCC Amateur Radio Licenses in Egan

Call Sign: KC0PME
Dennis E Lewis
100 E 2nd St
Egan SD 57024

Call Sign: KC0NFE
Donald C Simmons Jr
103 S Elm
Egan SD 57024

FCC Amateur Radio Licenses in Elk Point

Call Sign: WA0ARZ
R James Wennblom
47553 319th St
Elk Point SD 57025

Call Sign: K0HW
R James Wennblom
47553 319th St
Elk Point SD 57025

Call Sign: KE0IE
Thomas L Carlson
47437 320th St
Elk Point SD 57025

Call Sign: KB0ZQB
David J Fullenkamp
RR1
Elk Point SD 57025

Call Sign: N1BEJ
Alyson Grupp
Elk Point SD 57025

FCC Amateur Radio Licenses in Elkton

Call Sign: KC0PSR
Susan H Schuurman
513 Antelope St
Elkton SD 57026

Call Sign: KC0OFZ
Arend Schuurman
513 Antelope St
Elkton SD 57026

Call Sign: KC0TWO
Patty J Dexter
206 N Elk St
Elkton SD 57026

Call Sign: W0TKV
Harold G Smallfield
403 W 2nd St
Elkton SD 57026

Call Sign: KC0SKF
Craig A Dexter
Elkton SD 57026

Call Sign: KD0ECO
John C Nilles
Elkton SD 57026

Call Sign: KC0FFG
John E Bubach
Elkton SD 570260026

Call Sign: KB0OVY
Wayne R Williams
Elkton SD 570260275

FCC Amateur Radio Licenses in Ellsworth AFB

Call Sign: KD7HSL
Paul D Dejarnette
2630 Arnold Dr Unit 658

Ellsworth AFB SD 57706

Call Sign: KC0QFC
Jeffery S Toney
633 Beadle Ct
Ellsworth AFB SD 57706

Call Sign: KB0QAZ
Matthew T Insko
882 Dunn Ct
Ellsworth AFB SD 57706

Call Sign: KA5WMV
Henry J Eschmann III
23 Rim Rd
Ellsworth AFB SD 57706

FCC Amateur Radio Licenses in Emery

Call Sign: KA0VSR
Robert E Weber
130 7th St S
Emery SD 57332

Call Sign: KD0CAP
Arthur E Hoult
411 N 6th 858
Emery SD 57332

Call Sign: N7AEH
Arthur E Hoult
411 N 6th 858
Emery SD 57332

Call Sign: N0PCV
David R Giesler
411 N 6th St
Emery SD 57332

Call Sign: KA3KWM
Glenn B Knight
411 N 6th St 1436
Emery SD 57332

Call Sign: N3KNF
Beverly D Knight
411 N 6th St 1436
Emery SD 57332

Call Sign: N9HRH
Gerald R Brandt
411 N 6th St 1444
Emery SD 57332

Call Sign: W6POH
Donald H Gilbertsen
411 N 6th St 1489
Emery SD 573322124

Call Sign: KD0HAX
James J Heinen
411 N 6th St 1531
Emery SD 57332

Call Sign: K0WVN
Joe A Elliott
411 N 6th St 1801
Emery SD 57332

Call Sign: WA3Z
John D Hartman
411 N 6th St 1821
Emery SD 57332

Call Sign: WB3FXH
Janice K Hartman
411 N 6th St 1821
Emery SD 57332

Call Sign: N6KPX
Richard L Pipes Jr
411 N 6th St 205
Emery SD 57332

Call Sign: W4ET
Ronnie D Hutchison
411 N 6th St 2372
Emery SD 573322124

Call Sign: WA9PCI
Orvis L Wertz
411 N 6th St 2509
Emery SD 573322124

Call Sign: KB3CWZ
John A Hards
411 N 6th St 2700
Emery SD 57332

Call Sign: WB6DUN
Herman T Thiel III
411 N 6th St 3331
Emery SD 57332

Call Sign: KD0BOW
Kimball O Anderson
411 N 6th St 3801
Emery SD 57332

Call Sign: KD0GRK
Wilson Rogers
411 N 6th St 858
Emery SD 57332

Call Sign: WB1DAN
Mark B Grossman
411 N 6th St 939
Emery SD 57332

Call Sign: KC0AEQ
Helen E Giesler
411 N 6th St Pmb 2350
Emery SD 57332

Call Sign: KC0KLM
Lonnie G Schreiner
411 N 6th St Pmb 2493
Emery SD 573322124

Call Sign: KD0JYI
John R Pontsler
411 N 6th St Pmb 2663
Emery SD 57332

Call Sign: K3JRP
John R Pontsler
411 N 6th St Pmb 2663
Emery SD 57332

Call Sign: KD0QLH
Robert A Howland
411 N 6th St Pmb 3279
Emery SD 57332

Call Sign: K0VLJ
Sam Scherf
411 N 6th St Unit 655
Emery SD 573322124

Call Sign: N7OSR
William C Vassar
42837 SD Hwy 42 270
Emery SD 57332

Call Sign: KB7SSD
David E Jones
42837 SD Hwy 42 433
Emery SD 573327007

Call Sign: KC7DNV
Douglas M Maus
42837 SD Hwy 42 922
Emery SD 57332

FCC Amateur Radio Licenses in Estelline

Call Sign: KB0NB
Dwayne M Gorder
19052 471st Ave
Estelline SD 57234

Call Sign: KC0BUA
Andrew M Gorder
19052 471st Ave
Estelline SD 57234

Call Sign: KB0PZ
Sherry L Gorder

RR1
Estelline SD 57234

Call Sign: KB0CJB
Robert M Martin
RR1
Estelline SD 57234

Call Sign: N0YAD
Marceen A Nystrom
46609 SD Hwy 28
Estelline SD 57234

Call Sign: WD0GTU
David L Nystrom
46609 SD Hwy 28
Estelline SD 57234

FCC Amateur Radio Licenses in Eureka

Call Sign: N1KPL
Tony W Day
503 E Ave
Eureka SD 57437

Call Sign: KC0PDD
James E Lang
Eureka SD 57437

Call Sign: KC0SSF
Josephine K Lang
Eureka SD 574370545

FCC Amateur Radio Licenses in Fairview

Call Sign: N0JPE
Scot A Montgomery
320 Elm Box 53
Fairview SD 57027

Call Sign: KD0BEH
Don J London
619 Main St

Fairview SD 57027

Call Sign: KD0FGH
Alan D Reinpold
Fairview SD 57027

Call Sign: KD0BUG
Jeffrey J Roti
Fairview SD 57027

FCC Amateur Radio Licenses in Faith

Call Sign: AB5NA
Jay K Springman
Faith SD 57626

Call Sign: AC5PU
Carol I Pratt
Faith SD 576260054

FCC Amateur Radio Licenses in Faulkton

Call Sign: KC0YCA
Mark S Kleinsasser
15442 343rd Ave
Faulkton SD 57438

Call Sign: KB0NZD
Ben J Wurtz
Faulkton SD 57438

FCC Amateur Radio Licenses in Ferney

Call Sign: KA0EYW
Gregory L Pigors
Ferney SD 57439

FCC Amateur Radio Licenses in Flandreau

Call Sign: W0BKF
Lyle E Morrison

404 1st Ave E
Flandreau SD 57028

Call Sign: K9VKC
Stefan G Van Aalst
312 E Pipestone Ave
Flandreau SD 57028

Call Sign: KD0EUL
Terry G Albers
100 N Veterans St
Flandreau SD 57028

Call Sign: K0TGA
Terry G Albers
100 N Veterans St
Flandreau SD 57028

Call Sign: N0EQZ
Joel V Xavier
RR2
Flandreau SD 57028

Call Sign: WD0GFH
Floyd A Johnson
501 W 3rd Ave
Flandreau SD 57028

FCC Amateur Radio Licenses in Forestburg

Call Sign: AA0F
Donald K Schwemle
23464 404th Ave
Forestburg SD 57314

Call Sign: N0XDP
Jason E Nurnberg
HC 74
Forestburg SD 57314

Call Sign: KB0NGP
Jeremy M Hunter
HC 74
Forestburg SD 57314

Call Sign: N0XDN
Steve E Hunter
HC 74
Forestburg SD 57314

Call Sign: N0OTI
Douglas L Nurnberg
40406 SD Hwy 34
Forestburg SD 573146421

FCC Amateur Radio Licenses in Fort Pierre

Call Sign: KC7KFH
Gary L Dettman
27372 Bad River Rd
Fort Pierre SD 57532

Call Sign: KC0TRT
Gary L Dettman
27372 Bad River Rd
Fort Pierre SD 57532

Call Sign: KA0VTM
Leon K Rowell
HCR 32
Fort Pierre SD 57532

Call Sign: WB0NZU
Naomi K Boe
179 Islay Ave
Fort Pierre SD 57532

Call Sign: N0HNY
Steven D Stewart
209 S 6th St Box 705
Fort Pierre SD 57532

Call Sign: KD4WWU
Jonathan P Irwin
162 Skerrols St Apt C7
Fort Pierre SD 57532

Call Sign: KB0TLG

Jacquelyn F Eldridge
28169 US Hwy 14 34
Fort Pierre SD 57532

Call Sign: N0ZZU
Ralph J Eldridge
28169 US Hwy 14 34
Fort Pierre SD 57532

Call Sign: KB0PGW
Cheryl M Stoeser
412 W 2nd Ave Box 187
Fort Pierre SD 57532

Call Sign: KB0QVP
Lucas L Stoeser
412 W 2nd Ave Box 187
Fort Pierre SD 57532

Call Sign: KB0YXZ
David H Mehlhoff
2101 Waldron St
Fort Pierre SD 57532

Call Sign: W0NWT
David H Mehlhoff
2101 Waldron St
Fort Pierre SD 57532

Call Sign: KB0ATT
Bill Wilson
Fort Pierre SD 57532

Call Sign: KA0ZZY
Mark S Louder
Fort Pierre SD 57532

Call Sign: KC0KXS
Evan L Wempe
Fort Pierre SD 57532

FCC Amateur Radio Licenses in Fort Thompson

Call Sign: N0OZY

Douglas R Todd
Fort Thompson SD 57339

FCC Amateur Radio Licenses in Frankfort

Call Sign: N0PCW
Daniel J Enander
18231 398th Ave
Frankfort SD 57440

Call Sign: KB0ROS
Ruben L Enander
18239 398th Ave
Frankfort SD 57440

Call Sign: KB0IPY
Zane E Mason
17710 401st Ave
Frankfort SD 57440

FCC Amateur Radio Licenses in Frederick

Call Sign: KB0KMH
John L Noble
39038 114th St
Frederick SD 574416405

Call Sign: KD0NIL
Archie L Clifford Jr
37947 115th St
Frederick SD 57441

FCC Amateur Radio Licenses in Freeman

Call Sign: KA0DTU
Raymond J Becker
43861 276th St
Freeman SD 570296101

Call Sign: KC0ZU
Gregory A Kleinsasser
43639 277th St

Freeman SD 570296109

Call Sign: KC0BUB
Danielle R Stagman
27417 429 Ave
Freeman SD 57029

Call Sign: K0TPF
Frederick J Walz
27417 429th Ave
Freeman SD 57029

Call Sign: WB0VFP
Isaac C Unruh
724 Cherry St
Freeman SD 57029

Call Sign: W0GWA
Melvin L Hofer
312 E 3rd
Freeman SD 57029

Call Sign: N0LTK
Edwin J Jantzen
721 E 3rd St
Freeman SD 57029

Call Sign: KB0TOJ
Lori J Walz
RR1
Freeman SD 57029

Call Sign: KB9SMV
Walter A Salis
104 S Dewald St
Freeman SD 57029

Call Sign: W0EXX
Darius Hofer
Freeman SD 57029

Call Sign: N0SD
John R Waltner
Freeman SD 57029

FCC Amateur Radio Licenses in Fulton

Call Sign: KD0HBO
Jessica A Reed
41965 SD Hwy 38
Fulton SD 57340

Call Sign: KD0HBP
Jonathan R Reed
41965 SD Hwy 38
Fulton SD 57340

Call Sign: WA0CFC
Donald W O Neill
Fulton SD 57340

FCC Amateur Radio Licenses in Gann Valley

Call Sign: N0BME
John W Naser
SR 3
Gann Valley SD 57341

Call Sign: N0FNR
Mary L Naser
SR 3
Gann Valley SD 57341

FCC Amateur Radio Licenses in Garden City

Call Sign: K7OMK
Glen E Harding
325 E Main
Garden City SD 57236

Call Sign: KA0EYV
Ralph R Hartley
Rt 1
Garden City SD 57236

Call Sign: KB0GDI
Helen M Harding

Garden City SD 57236

FCC Amateur Radio Licenses in Garretson

Call Sign: KE0RJ
Dale H Bower
25225 479th Ave
Garretson SD 57030

Call Sign: N0PEJ
Susan M Bower
25225 479th Ave
Garretson SD 57030

Call Sign: N8KCL
Gary M Shonkwiler
25433 487th Ave
Garretson SD 570306103

Call Sign: N1FTJ
Brian T Parr
1008 4th St
Garretson SD 57030

Call Sign: KD0DOM
Brian T Parr
1008 4th St
Garretson SD 57030

Call Sign: KE7DME
Billie D Asay
508 Royce
Garretson SD 57030

Call Sign: KC0JZM
Michelle M Albers
Garretson SD 57030

FCC Amateur Radio Licenses in Gary

Call Sign: KA0REM
Lisa L Thomas
48536 183rd St
Gary SD 57237

Call Sign: KC0UO
James L Cleveland
48715 185th St
Gary SD 57237

Call Sign: W0GC
Gary C Carlson
2566 Lake Cochrane Dr W
Gary SD 572375518

Call Sign: KB0GMZ
Tim R Kloos
RR1
Gary SD 57237

Call Sign: N0NVS
Lee Ann M Kloos
RR1
Gary SD 57237

FCC Amateur Radio Licenses in Geddes

Call Sign: KA0VYT
Daniel J Stuart
603 S Main Ave
Geddes SD 57342

FCC Amateur Radio Licenses in Gettysburg

Call Sign: KC0DSB
Bruce W Schreiber
17209 301st Ave
Gettysburg SD 574429303

Call Sign: W0JR
Jesse Rausch
17181 302 Ave
Gettysburg SD 57442

Call Sign: WA0WAS
Gene A Horn
905 E Logan Ave

Gettysburg SD 574421627

Call Sign: KD0GEE
Angela S Freidel
513 Holly Dr
Gettysburg SD 57442

Call Sign: KD0GEC
Kelly A Lockwood
513 Holly Dr
Gettysburg SD 57442

FCC Amateur Radio Licenses in Glenham

Call Sign: N0YFH
Philip M Salem
29533 129St
Glenham SD 57631

Call Sign: KD0JJK
Roger P Salem
Glenham SD 57631

FCC Amateur Radio Licenses in Goodwin

Call Sign: KC0GSC
Jarred W Stohr
17924 465 Ave
Goodwin SD 57238

FCC Amateur Radio Licenses in Gregory

Call Sign: K0VI
William J Schreiner
806 Church Ave
Gregory SD 57533

FCC Amateur Radio Licenses in Grenville

Call Sign: KB0CRL

Corey T Liknes
RR1
Grenville SD 57239

Call Sign: KD0NIP
Daniel P Riley
1023 Y Camp Rd
Grenville SD 57239

Call Sign: W0UGM
Daniel P Riley
1023 Y Camp Rd
Grenville SD 57239

FCC Amateur Radio Licenses in Groton

Call Sign: W0OYQ
Robert A Peterson
608 N 2nd St
Groton SD 57445

FCC Amateur Radio Licenses in Harrisburg

Call Sign: KB9WAW
Diane F Whelan
27194 479th Ave
Harrisburg SD 57032

Call Sign: KA0HMO
William M Childs
414 Cypress Cir
Harrisburg SD 57032

Call Sign: KB0FTS
Barton J Van Heuveln
607 Maple St
Harrisburg SD 57032

Call Sign: KA0WOF
Randy A Tassler
608 S Grand
Harrisburg SD 57032

Call Sign: N0VYP
Dennis M Vickerman
Harrisburg SD 57032

FCC Amateur Radio Licenses in Hartford

Call Sign: KC0MAZ
Michael W Clark
45979 253rd St
Hartford SD 57033

Call Sign: KD0FGG
Eric R Larsen
25421 461st Ave
Hartford SD 57033

Call Sign: KD0RHD
James H Anderson
208 Crestwood Dr
Hartford SD 57033

Call Sign: W0CSB
Wayne C Freeburg
26567 E Shore Pl
Hartford SD 570336718

Call Sign: KC0WZD
Nick N Hamze
46516 Kloxin Dr
Hartford SD 57033

Call Sign: N0DPF
Matthias S Spisak
200 N Mundt
Hartford SD 570332237

Call Sign: WB0ACV
Timothy J Graham
301 Sagehorn Dr
Hartford SD 57033

FCC Amateur Radio Licenses in Hayti

Call Sign: N0GVM
Randall D Frederick
18806 446th Ave
Hayti SD 57241

Call Sign: KB0WYG
Thomas L Stein
408 Redbird Ave
Hayti SD 57241

Call Sign: WB0TJY
Jacob J Sprang
503 Redbird Ave
Hayti SD 57241

Call Sign: KD6PWU
Clifford I Skaalen
RR1
Hayti SD 57241

Call Sign: KE0WK
Larry N Haaland
Hayti SD 57241

Call Sign: KD0LJG
David D Schaefer
Hayti SD 57241

FCC Amateur Radio Licenses in Hecla

Call Sign: KD0JZF
Scott N Stearns
10143 397th Ave
Hecla SD 57446

FCC Amateur Radio Licenses in Henry

Call Sign: KF0YX
Boyd E Joens
17413 436th Ave
Henry SD 57243

Call Sign: KB0JOC

Kenneth E Luvaas
413 S Elm St
Henry SD 57243

FCC Amateur Radio Licenses in Hermosa

Call Sign: W6GLK
Ray L Foster
13839 Battle Creek Rd
Hermosa SD 57744

Call Sign: N6RWN
Frances L Foster
13839 Battle Creek Rd
Hermosa SD 577440019

Call Sign: WB7BYG
Stanley W Hixson
24697 Bender Ridge Rd
Hermosa SD 57744

Call Sign: KB2JX
Robert J Trefz
HCR 89
Hermosa SD 57744

Call Sign: N0RHQ
Luther L Trefz
HCR 89
Hermosa SD 57744

Call Sign: KD0MVX
Norman H Christopherson
150 Main St
Hermosa SD 57744

Call Sign: KC9FAU
Andrew M Tate
14044 Paha Sapa Dr
Hermosa SD 57744

Call Sign: KC0WEV
Cindy L Tate
14044 Paha Sapa Dr

Hermosa SD 577447004

Call Sign: KD0CZW
Allen L Tate
14044 Paha Sapa Dr
Hermosa SD 57744

Call Sign: KD0DZJ
Dick W Deutscher
13805 SD Hwy 40
Hermosa SD 57744

Call Sign: K0DEU
Dick W Deutscher
13805 SD Hwy 40
Hermosa SD 57744

Call Sign: KD0QCH
Susan E Deutscher
13805 SD Hwy 40
Hermosa SD 57744

Call Sign: K1SED
Susan E Deutscher
13805 SD Hwy 40
Hermosa SD 57744

Call Sign: KD4DXX
Karin K Thompson
Hermosa SD 57744

Call Sign: KU4HP
Rod M Thompson
Hermosa SD 57744

Call Sign: KD0NGM
Brittany M Nunez
Hermosa SD 57744

FCC Amateur Radio Licenses in Herreid

Call Sign: KD0JZG
Nick L Berndt
Herreid SD 57632

FCC Amateur Radio Licenses in Highmore

Call Sign: AD7BA
Michael D Bryan
316 Commercial Ave SE
Highmore SD 57345

Call Sign: N0ICW
Michael D Bryan
316 Commercial Ave SE
Highmore SD 57345

Call Sign: KB0EYA
John J Sleger
Highmore SD 57345

Call Sign: KC0AF
James M Whipple
Highmore SD 57345

Call Sign: N0WRP
Adeline H Whipple
Highmore SD 57345

FCC Amateur Radio Licenses in Hill City

Call Sign: KC7LXA
Frank S Garcia
111 Elm St
Hill City SD 57745

Call Sign: KB0DOI
Bruce F Johnson
12551 Ford Mtn Ct
Hill City SD 577450475

Call Sign: KB0MCM
Joseph G Tippmann
Hill City
Hill City SD 57745

Call Sign: N0JPS

Joe C Hogg
SR Box 86A
Hill City SD 57745

Call Sign: N0NDA
Robert C Marx
Hill City SD 57745

Call Sign: N0YOJ
David K Blansett
Hill City SD 57745

Call Sign: N0YOK
Angie D Blansett
Hill City SD 57745

Call Sign: W4PBU
Winfield D Henry
Hill City SD 57745

Call Sign: W0MZI
Frances H Kruse
Hill City SD 57745

Call Sign: KB0UYO
William E Dohr
Hill City SD 57745

Call Sign: N0DUW
Karen F Kruse
Hill City SD 57745

Call Sign: N0DUX
Harold A Kruse
Hill City SD 57745

Call Sign: KC0QJY
Rodger L Marx
Hill City SD 57745

Call Sign: W8CG
Charles R Landon Jr
Hill City SD 577450911

Call Sign: KE0UV

Gregory R Mc Intire
Hill City SD 577451045

FCC Amateur Radio Licenses in Hitchcock

Call Sign: W0PMA
Bert C Stewart
329 Cherry St Box 115
Hitchcock SD 57348

Call Sign: WA0PNB
Norval F Goehring
131 Maple Ave
Hitchcock SD 573482007

Call Sign: N0VWZ
Dewey L Minske
Hitchcock SD 57348

FCC Amateur Radio Licenses in Hot Springs

Call Sign: KD0GEF
Ted P Ebert
538 Albany Ave
Hot Springs SD 57747

Call Sign: KB0AKL
Hannah I Swartz
1801 Albany Ave
Hot Springs SD 57747

Call Sign: KD0AAF
Joseph R Birdsall
2204 Albany Ave
Hot Springs SD 57747

Call Sign: W0HGZ
Dwight H Sholl
1602 Baltimore Ave
Hot Springs SD 57747

Call Sign: KB0ZVP
Todd A Hills

2209 Baltimore Ave
Hot Springs SD 57747

Call Sign: KB0ZVS
Krista K Hills
2209 Baltimore Ave
Hot Springs SD 57747

Call Sign: N0KKK
Krista K Hills
2209 Baltimore Ave
Hot Springs SD 57747

Call Sign: AC0PN
Bruno Busslinger
522 Bear Ave
Hot Springs SD 57747

Call Sign: N0TJG
Dean J Tinaglia
27622 Brook Dr
Hot Springs SD 57747

Call Sign: KF4XP
William J Parman
26751 Buffalo Butte Rd
Hot Springs SD 57747

Call Sign: KC0WIC
William M Martin
309 Canton Ave
Hot Springs SD 57747

Call Sign: N0VZO
Stephen P Niemann
1212 Canton Ave
Hot Springs SD 57747

Call Sign: KB0KIK
Travis P Merkel
1746 Canton Ave
Hot Springs SD 57747

Call Sign: KC0AFU
Sheryl F Malde

27993 Cascade Rd
Hot Springs SD 57747

Call Sign: N0SWK
Brian L Malde
27993 Cascade Rd
Hot Springs SD 57747

Call Sign: KA0FUH
John E Renstrom
1546 Catholiean Ave
Hot Springs SD 57747

Call Sign: KD0DZI
Jon A Nabholz
13161 Cougar Pass Rd
Hot Springs SD 57747

Call Sign: KD0DZH
Roland P Nabholz
13161 Cougar Pass Rd
Hot Springs SD 57747

Call Sign: KB0AKJ
Winfield A Pengra
401 Dakota
Hot Springs SD 57747

Call Sign: KA0FTB
Desmond Mitchard
206 Dakota St
Hot Springs SD 57747

Call Sign: KB0KNI
Jo Cunningham
1838 Detroit
Hot Springs SD 57747

Call Sign: KA0FUI
Phillip G Knapp
1809 Detroit Ave Box 173
Hot Springs SD 57747

Call Sign: W0FUI
Phillip G Knapp

1809 Detroit Ave Box 173
Hot Springs SD 57747

27612 Garden Dr
Hot Springs SD 57747

Call Sign: N0SXX
Gary D Slagel
2226 Doran Rd
Hot Springs SD 57747

Call Sign: N0XJE
Roger D Hubregtse
HC 52
Hot Springs SD 57747

Call Sign: KT0A
Gary D Slagel
2226 Doran Rd
Hot Springs SD 57747

Call Sign: KB0KNH
Teresa A Campbell
HC 52
Hot Springs SD 57747

Call Sign: K0HS
Hot Springs Amateur Radio Club
2226 Duran Rd
Hot Springs SD 57747

Call Sign: KB0KPQ
Anne M Campbell
HC 52
Hot Springs SD 57747

Call Sign: KD0DUE
Penny S Hanna
12912 Evans Loop
Hot Springs SD 57747

Call Sign: KB0LHV
Emily S Campbell
HC 52
Hot Springs SD 57747

Call Sign: KC0WEU
Billy E Beeman
1513 Evans St
Hot Springs SD 577473026

Call Sign: KB0KNK
Matt A Campbell
HC 52
Hot Springs SD 57747

Call Sign: N0THB
Robert J Beninati
1549 Evanston Ave
Hot Springs SD 57747

Call Sign: N0THA
D Keith Miller
HCR 52
Hot Springs SD 57747

Call Sign: KA0SIN
Glen R Anderson
13196 Fall River Rd
Hot Springs SD 57747

Call Sign: WD0DWS
Daniel P Pucket
HCR 52
Hot Springs SD 57747

Call Sign: KC0PJM
Elaine L Anderson
13196 Fall River Rd
Hot Springs SD 57747

Call Sign: KA0ICH
Trudy K Renstrom
HCR 52
Hot Springs SD 57747

Call Sign: WA0FGV
Arthur M Mower

Call Sign: N0SWM
Amy L Pucket

HCR 52
Hot Springs SD 57747

440 N 20th St
Hot Springs SD 57747

Call Sign: W0LFB
Lois M Grundstrom
27773 Himmel Wright Rd
Hot Springs SD 57747

Call Sign: W0MAT
Matt E Anderson
440 N 20th St
Hot Springs SD 57747

Call Sign: W7LFB
Roger D Grundstrom
27773 Himmel Wright Rd
Hot Springs SD 57747

Call Sign: W0PAM
Pamela J Anderson
440 N 20th St
Hot Springs SD 57747

Call Sign: N0CNS
Theodore R Jacobson
2001 Lincoln
Hot Springs SD 57747

Call Sign: K0OR
Timothy L Anderson
440 N 20th St
Hot Springs SD 577471515

Call Sign: KD0NYI
Robert W Puffer
2233 Lincoln Ave
Hot Springs SD 57747

Call Sign: W7VOK
Larry R Witt
717 N 23
Hot Springs SD 57747

Call Sign: KB0ZVQ
Gwen A Healey
27364 Memorial Rd
Hot Springs SD 57747

Call Sign: KC0WIA
Joshua E Tatum
345 N 5th St
Hot Springs SD 57747

Call Sign: WA0TMI
George B Bragg
2500 Minnekahta Ave
Hot Springs SD 57747

Call Sign: KC0KBU
Larry R Witt
710 NW River
Hot Springs SD 57747

Call Sign: KD0NYJ
Michael S Randle
2500 Minnekahta Ave
Hot Springs SD 57747

Call Sign: KA4PJV
John L Safris Sr
702 NW River St
Hot Springs SD 57747

Call Sign: N7ITW
Robert L Seaboldt
11981 Mt Lion Lane
Hot Springs SD 57747

Call Sign: KI6JUD
Linda G Weed
27452 Pass Rd
Hot Springs SD 57747

Call Sign: KC0AFS
Pamela J Anderson

Call Sign: WS0V
Alonzo B Seaboldt

27461 Pass Rd
Hot Springs SD 57747

544 S 16th St
Hot Springs SD 57747

Call Sign: WA3DYT
Robert A Goldberg
12691 Ridgeview Dr
Hot Springs SD 57747

Call Sign: N0SWN
Mark A Goesch
246 S 19th St
Hot Springs SD 57747

Call Sign: KC0KBV
Ari Juhala
RR 1
Hot Springs SD 57747

Call Sign: WB0LTV
Le Roy E Smith
238 S 5th St
Hot Springs SD 57747

Call Sign: W0BSC
Battle Mountain Amateur Radio Clb
RR1
Hot Springs SD 57747

Call Sign: N0XOF
Franklin L Flyte
105 S 6th St
Hot Springs SD 57747

Call Sign: N0XYG
Darlene E Seaboldt
RR1
Hot Springs SD 57747

Call Sign: KA0UDM
Eve A English
309 S 6th St
Hot Springs SD 57747

Call Sign: NB0D
Helen J Stephan
RR1
Hot Springs SD 57747

Call Sign: W0EDV
Jesse E English
309 S 6th St
Hot Springs SD 57747

Call Sign: KC0KBX
Susan K Burden
Rt 1
Hot Springs SD 57747

Call Sign: KC0QXU
Ronald A Pyle
1140 S 6th St 1
Hot Springs SD 57747

Call Sign: KC0KBY
Brett L Burden
Rt 1
Hot Springs SD 57747

Call Sign: KI0PG
Lynn W Finch
610 University Ave
Hot Springs SD 57747

Call Sign: N0VZN
Aaron B Wear
509 S 15th St
Hot Springs SD 57747

Call Sign: KD0DLB
Kelly J Campbell
314 Valley View Dr
Hot Springs SD 57747

Call Sign: N0KHT
Kevin L Bowker

Call Sign: KC0KBZ
Robert A Ikonen

28612 W Southshore Rd
Hot Springs SD 57747

Call Sign: KB0KIV
Robert H Fridell
1601 Washington
Hot Springs SD 57747

Call Sign: N0VZM
Les T Hanson
1746 Washington Ave
Hot Springs SD 57747

Call Sign: KA0WZE
Lori J Anderson
2145 Washington Ave
Hot Springs SD 57747

Call Sign: N0IWR
John Anderson
2145 Washington Ave
Hot Springs SD 57747

Call Sign: W9LEQ
Carl H Anderson
2145 Washington Ave
Hot Springs SD 57747

Call Sign: KB0DVI
Thomas B Wozniak
1729 Wilson Ave
Hot Springs SD 57747

Call Sign: KB0DVJ
Luke D Wozniak
1729 Wilson Ave
Hot Springs SD 57747

Call Sign: KC0WET
Matthew O Luebeck
2531 Wilson Ave
Hot Springs SD 57747

Call Sign: KC0KBW
Marlene M Akhtar

27123 Wind Cave Rd
Hot Springs SD 577477532

Call Sign: KC0KND
Hasan Akhtar
27123 Wind Cave Rd
Hot Springs SD 577477532

Call Sign: KC0WIB
John C Davis
27123 Wind Cave Rd
Hot Springs SD 57747

Call Sign: KA0FNH
Willis W Howard
Hot Springs SD 57747

Call Sign: N0IQS
John L Prall
Hot Springs SD 57747

Call Sign: N0SWL
Lois A Prall
Hot Springs SD 57747

Call Sign: N0VYN
Tristan J Clements
Hot Springs SD 57747

Call Sign: N0VZL
Scott R Worrall
Hot Springs SD 57747

Call Sign: WZ0W
Ronald H Brown
Hot Springs SD 57747

Call Sign: KB0UQH
School Radio Club
Hot Springs SD 57747

Call Sign: KA0IGV
Susan L Knapp
Hot Springs SD 57747

Call Sign: KB0UWC
Roger A Koppes
Hot Springs SD 57747

Call Sign: KE0WM
David A Longacre
Hot Springs SD 57747

Call Sign: WU0H
D Keith Doughty
Hot Springs SD 57747

Call Sign: KC0WID
Robert E Phares
Hot Springs SD 57747

Call Sign: KA0ROB
Robert E Phares
Hot Springs SD 57747

Call Sign: W0IGV
Susan L Knapp
Hot Springs SD 57747

Call Sign: NC0K
Thomas B Embree
Hot Springs SD 57747

FCC Amateur Radio Licenses in Howard

Call Sign: KB0WSZ
Robert K Thompson
705 E Farmer Ave
Howard SD 57349

FCC Amateur Radio Licenses in Hudson

Call Sign: KA0BZV
Donald L Simonson
620 Harris St
Hudson SD 57034

Call Sign: KC0RMR

Nicholas A Blake
819 Hubbard St
Hudson SD 57034

FCC Amateur Radio Licenses in Hurley

Call Sign: KB0VVZ
Paul J Balzer
44733 284th St
Hurley SD 57036

Call Sign: KI0AJ
Charles W Graham
Hurley SD 57036

FCC Amateur Radio Licenses in Huron

Call Sign: WD0DBI
Lewis F Schaar
819 12th St SW
Huron SD 57350

Call Sign: KB0NAA
Craig H Johnson
579 13th St SW
Huron SD 57350

Call Sign: WA0TKX
Robert D Johnson
280 18th St SE
Huron SD 57350

Call Sign: KB0LBU
Robert D Wullweber
612 18th St SW
Huron SD 57350

Call Sign: N0VYQ
Dwight A Wullweber
612 18th St SW
Huron SD 57350

Call Sign: KC0SQW

Jay R Winter
39704 212th St
Huron SD 57350

Call Sign: K0OH
Jack W Winter
39704 212th St
Huron SD 573506520

Call Sign: N0ZPC
Jochen Kolb
139 22nd St SW
Huron SD 57350

Call Sign: KC2RHV
Bernard P Keeler
708 27th St NE
Huron SD 57350

Call Sign: KC7UPJ
Richard J January Jr
21407 396th Ave
Huron SD 573507501

Call Sign: K0HHZ
Donald E Winter
21221 397 Ave
Huron SD 573506519

Call Sign: KB0MZZ
Marina T Pappas
366 3rd St SE
Huron SD 573502504

Call Sign: KB0VTS
Ernst L Scheinert
179 4th St NE
Huron SD 57350

Call Sign: KB0ROU
Debra K Brock
381 5th St NE
Huron SD 57350

Call Sign: N0NKH

Douglas A Brock
381 5th St NE
Huron SD 57350

Call Sign: KC0CZO
Harlin E Rada
1818 Arizona Ave SW Apt 316
Huron SD 57350

Call Sign: K0JMW
Owen S Johnson
631 Beach Ave SE
Huron SD 57350

Call Sign: WA0CKH
Roland L Thompson
817 Colorado SW
Huron SD 57350

Call Sign: KB0TP
David D Dorris
22 Columbia Ave SE
Huron SD 57350

Call Sign: KB0ROV
Peter J Mahowald
628 Dakota Ave S
Huron SD 57350

Call Sign: WA0TDK
William W Kerker
4323 Dakota Ave S
Huron SD 573506539

Call Sign: KC0IXE
Todd J Madden
162 Dakota Ave S 4
Huron SD 57350

Call Sign: N0OTP
Denis J Mahowald
628 Dakota S
Huron SD 57350

Call Sign: N0OTB

Harold S Wipf
1119 Frank Ave SE
Huron SD 57350

Call Sign: KA0EJG
Jean R Pastian
705 Frank SE
Huron SD 57350

Call Sign: KD0NSD
Jeffrey D Emmert
1331 Idaho Ave SE
Huron SD 57350

Call Sign: AE0SD
Jeffrey D Emmert
1331 Idaho Ave SE
Huron SD 57350

Call Sign: K0HQD
Evelyn N Dugdale
668 Illinois Ave NW
Huron SD 573504622

Call Sign: KB0NAB
Philip P Wollman
1453 Iowa Ave SE
Huron SD 57350

Call Sign: KB0ROR
Gerald D Van Der Aarde
1157 Kansas Ave NE
Huron SD 57350

Call Sign: KC0DKA
Delbert W Moke
555 Kansas NE
Huron SD 57350

Call Sign: KC0KPR
Mary A Moke
555 Kansas NE
Huron SD 57350

Call Sign: KC0BAR

Richard M Phillips
806 Kansas SE
Huron SD 57350

Call Sign: WA0NHJ
Charles J Mahowald
1003 Lawnridge
Huron SD 57350

Call Sign: N0JLS
Randall V Hoscheid
1830 Maple Dr SE
Huron SD 57350

Call Sign: W0MGH
John E Trinko
1039 Montana Ave SW
Huron SD 57350

Call Sign: KC0CAR
Douglas D Van Marel
680 Montana SW 108
Huron SD 57350

Call Sign: KD0LJ
Robert L Ost
618 Oregon Ave SE
Huron SD 573502829

Call Sign: KC0KGD
Melinda L Ellenson
670 Oregon Ave SE
Huron SD 57350

Call Sign: KB0VYR
Michael B Hughes
1075 Parkside Dr SW
Huron SD 57350

Call Sign: KB0ROW
Lee A Hildman
1718 Simmons SE
Huron SD 57350

Call Sign: N7EOK

Scott E Mallard
260 Sunrise Dr
Huron SD 57350

Call Sign: KM0F
William W Kerker
920 West Park Ave NW
Huron SD 57350

Call Sign: K0GZV
Herbert J Bandelman
722 Wisc SW
Huron SD 57350

Call Sign: WA0ZXV
Raymond C Lang
2207 Wisconsin Ave SW
Huron SD 57350

Call Sign: W0ILL
Edward R Mathews
Huron SD 57350

Call Sign: W0SOV
Marie C Mathews
Huron SD 57350

Call Sign: KA0ZZG
Margret A Albertz
Huron SD 57350

Call Sign: W0NOZ
Huron Amateur Radio Club
Huron SD 57350

Call Sign: WB0UTI
John North
Huron SD 57350

Call Sign: WB0ULX
Lloyd V Timperley Jr
Huron SD 573500205

FCC Amateur Radio Licenses in Ipswitch

Call Sign: KB0IUS
Jason J Heintzman
35641 135th St
Ipswich SD 57451

Call Sign: WA0ZPT
Dwain E Gibson
Ipswich SD 57451

Call Sign: KC7PVV
Roger R Gardner
Ipswich SD 57451

Call Sign: K0CRD
Myron A Fillbach
Ipswich SD 57451

FCC Amateur Radio Licenses in Iroquois

Call Sign: W3KP
Dennis A Aughenbaugh
221 Quapaw St
Iroquois SD 57353

Call Sign: W0SDK
Burdette C Aughenbaugh
RR1
Iroquois SD 57353

FCC Amateur Radio Licenses in Isabel

Call Sign: KB0MTG
Frances E Rollason
400 N Monroe
Isabel SD 57633

Call Sign: WA9WER
John A Ruege Sr
Isabel SD 57633

Call Sign: KC0LI
David H Rollason Jr

Isabel SD 57633

FCC Amateur Radio Licenses in Java

Call Sign: KB0WJM
Ralph E Bond
Java SD 574520036

FCC Amateur Radio Licenses in Jefferson

Call Sign: WB0IJV
Lois E Harkness
33138 479th Ave
Jefferson SD 57038

Call Sign: WB0VWO
Lee L Harkness
33138 479th Ave
Jefferson SD 57038

Call Sign: KC0GSV
Gary E Schaeffer
512 Division
Jefferson SD 57038

Call Sign: KB0DZW
Steve E Lofshult
Lakeshore Dr
Jefferson SD 57038

Call Sign: KC0FEM
Kevin J Connors
903 Shannon Dr
Jefferson SD 57038

Call Sign: KC0FJT
Isaac D Real
Jefferson SD 57038

FCC Amateur Radio Licenses in Kamloops

Call Sign: WB7PJR
Charles A Hays

8829 Westsyde Rd
Kamloops SD 57702

FCC Amateur Radio Licenses in Kennebec

Call Sign: WD0EDS
Judson W Huston
31234 232nd St
Kennebec SD 575445101

Call Sign: WB0PAI
Robert R Hills
Kennebec SD 575440305

FCC Amateur Radio Licenses in Keystone

Call Sign: KB7EDH
James Halley Jr
HCR 33
Keystone SD 57751

Call Sign: K0IX
Stephen J Hohman
24479 Oak Meadows Ct
Keystone SD 57751

Call Sign: N7HBK
Patricia A Wheaton
24479 Oak Meadows Ct
Keystone SD 57751

Call Sign: KM5A
Stephen M Wheaton
24479 Oak Meadows Ct
Keystone SD 577516658

Call Sign: KB0HLA
Ronald C Eilefson
13662 Pasque Flower Ct
Keystone SD 57751

FCC Amateur Radio Licenses in Kimball

Call Sign: N0EGJ
Betty R Burkine
Rt 2
Kimball SD 57355

FCC Amateur Radio Licenses in Lake Andes

Call Sign: N9ENE
Erin K Jones
RR2
Lake Andes SD 57356

FCC Amateur Radio Licenses in Lake City

Call Sign: KA0KKY
Kent L Duerre
116749 Roykota Dr
Lake City SD 57247

FCC Amateur Radio Licenses in Lake Norden

Call Sign: WA0MQK
Erland W Juntunen
Lake Norden SD 57248

FCC Amateur Radio Licenses in Lead

Call Sign: WB6GHA
John L Burch
55 2nd St
Lead SD 577541011

Call Sign: W0KTL
Donald S Sanders
109 3rd St
Lead SD 57754

Call Sign: KD6LAP
George F Laun
217 Deer Path
Lead SD 577541015

Call Sign: KE6KQZ
Thelma F Laun
217 Deer Path
Lead SD 577541015

Call Sign: N0LAP
George F Laun
217 Deer Path
Lead SD 577541015

Call Sign: KC0HIC
Rodger L Marx
209 Deer Path Rd
Lead SD 57754

Call Sign: KC0ZDA
Carol L Katz
309 E Summit
Lead SD 57754

Call Sign: W0APL
Edward E Fredrickson
504 Grand Ave
Lead SD 577542003

Call Sign: N0PFS
Jamey L Tollefson
608 Houston
Lead SD 57754

Call Sign: KC0ETG
Melanie L Tollefson
608 Houston St
Lead SD 577541239

Call Sign: KA0DIO
Duane A Ennis
121 May St
Lead SD 57754

Call Sign: KB0UYN
Michael S Tesch
8 N Galena St Apt 205

Lead SD 577541340

Call Sign: KD7PBK
Michael D Key
404 Sawyer St
Lead SD 57754

Call Sign: KD0JLU
Jeffery L Schroeder
804 W Mcclellan
Lead SD 57754

Call Sign: W0OZJ
Harold E Ross
Lead SD 57754

Call Sign: KA8HWT
William A Butler Sr
Lead SD 57754

FCC Amateur Radio Licenses in Lemmon

Call Sign: KC0GLC
Brent A David
602 1st Ave W
Lemmon SD 57638

Call Sign: KA0OTX
Fred F Huber
19 E 8th St
Lemmon SD 57639

FCC Amateur Radio Licenses in Lennox

Call Sign: WA0QMV
Floyd B Gulbrandson Jr
46643 278th St
Lennox SD 570395342

Call Sign: KC0MVE
Kevin C Booker
46352 279th St
Lennox SD 57039

Call Sign: N0HSS
Theresa M Gravning
46389 280th St
Lennox SD 57039

Call Sign: KC0JZP
Stacy E Gravning
46389 280th St
Lennox SD 57039

Call Sign: N0HRV
Don H Erks
720 S Main
Lennox SD 57039

Call Sign: W0BQH
Harold E Schneiderman
217 S Pine St 2
Lennox SD 570392105

Call Sign: KB0TOM
Mark E Luvaas
621 W 1st Ave
Lennox SD 57039

Call Sign: KA0HRD
Ernest L Cressman
Lennox SD 57039

Call Sign: KC0AE
Roland F Arlton
Lennox SD 57039

FCC Amateur Radio Licenses in Lesterville

Call Sign: KI0LM
Elmer A Mutschelknaus
29613 430th Ave
Lesterville SD 570405022

Call Sign: WB0TPV
Erna V Mutschelknaus
29613 430th Ave

Lesterville SD 570405022

FCC Amateur Radio Licenses in Letcher

Call Sign: KA0HON
Oscar C Thompson
39210 241st St
Letcher SD 57359

FCC Amateur Radio Licenses in Madison

Call Sign: N0XQG
Perry E Killion
45360 241st St
Madison SD 57042

Call Sign: N0VYR
Fawn C Killion
45360 241st St
Madison SD 57042

Call Sign: KF4AWX
Judith A Tarpley
23967 451st Ave
Madison SD 57042

Call Sign: WD4RNP
James W Tarpley
23967 451st Ave
Madison SD 57042

Call Sign: W0ZFH
James N Enga
23879 455th Ave
Madison SD 57042

Call Sign: KB0MRG
James C Enga
23879 455th Ave
Madison SD 57042

Call Sign: KC5TXD
Gwyneth C Palmer

110 Center St 1992
Madison SD 57042

Call Sign: KT4ET
Bruce E Palmer
110 Center St 1992
Madison SD 57042

Call Sign: KD0FWZ
Robert J Bragg
110 E Center Sr Pmb 653
Madison SD 57042

Call Sign: KF4NHJ
Dorothy A Carlton
110 E Center St
Madison SD 57042

Call Sign: KS4OJ
Joseph F Carlton Jr
110 E Center St
Madison SD 57042

Call Sign: KA1HB
Robert M Bligh
110 E Center St
Madison SD 57042

Call Sign: KC2JUS
Steven P St Germain
110 E Center St 1171
Madison SD 57042

Call Sign: KB2AAA
Steven P St Germain
110 E Center St 1171
Madison SD 57042

Call Sign: AC0VL
Steven P St Germain
110 E Center St 1171
Madison SD 57042

Call Sign: AG0B
Steven P St Germain

110 E Center St 1171
Madison SD 57042

Call Sign: W0SPS
Steven P St Germain
110 E Center St 1171
Madison SD 57042

Call Sign: KD7FEA
Jalone F Schaeffler
110 E Center St 1277
Madison SD 57042

Call Sign: AD7IE
Norman E Schaeffler
110 E Center St 1277
Madison SD 570422908

Call Sign: WB6QKL
Ralph E Vaden
110 E Center St 1487
Madison SD 57042

Call Sign: KA1ROI
Stephen J Loftus
110 E Center St 1634
Madison SD 57042

Call Sign: KD0QVM
Brian D Gifford
110 E Center St 1648
Madison SD 57042

Call Sign: N6ZCA
Larry G Emmons
110 E Center St 1724
Madison SD 57042

Call Sign: K0YUD
Charles H Larsen
110 E Center St 273
Madison SD 57042

Call Sign: KD4P
Peter L Hendrick

110 E Center St 422
Madison SD 57042

Call Sign: K4GLU
William A Merriman
110 E Center St 484
Madison SD 57042

Call Sign: KD0GXN
Cherie L Ve Ard
110 E Center St 614
Madison SD 570422908

Call Sign: KD0GXO
Chistopher M Dunphy
110 E Center St 614
Madison SD 570422908

Call Sign: KB1ES
Gary A Bismack
110 E Center St 811
Madison SD 57042

Call Sign: KC9JLV
James W Kane
110 E Center St 850
Madison SD 57042

Call Sign: WO0B
James W Kane
110 E Center St 850
Madison SD 57042

Call Sign: KC2RDE
Dawn C Houze-Nelson
110 E Center St 903
Madison SD 57042

Call Sign: W2ACY
Richard Nelson
110 E Center St 903
Madison SD 57042

Call Sign: KG4LRB
Vicki I Twining

110 E Center St Pmb 1062
Madison SD 570422908

Call Sign: W4RET
Ronald E Twining
110 E Center St Pmb 1062
Madison SD 570422908

Call Sign: AC0NM
Glenn R Sirkis
110 E Center St Pmb 870
Madison SD 570422908

Call Sign: KA8ZZK
Edward E Behnke
110 E Center St Pmb1283
Madison SD 57042

Call Sign: KC0TQX
Michael R Stunes
1100 N Harth Ave 4
Madison SD 57042

Call Sign: KA0JDN
David J Smith
512 N Josephine Ave
Madison SD 57042

Call Sign: KB0OUE
Jayson D Limmer
913 NE 10th St
Madison SD 57042

Call Sign: KA9ZJR
Owen K Bundy
913 NE 11th St
Madison SD 57042

Call Sign: KB0MCY
Warren W Uecker
904 NE 5th St
Madison SD 57042

Call Sign: W0DCO
Garold D Slagel

913 NE 9th St
Madison SD 57042

Call Sign: N0EJQ
Norman L Cummins
1026 NE Sixth St
Madison SD 57042

Call Sign: N0CTG
Robert L Zerfas
613 NW 2nd
Madison SD 570420087

Call Sign: NF2J
Clarence B De Weese
RR2
Madison SD 57042

Call Sign: K0ACF
Howard E Wick
619 SW 2nd St
Madison SD 57042

Call Sign: KC0LRU
Mark A O Loughlen
1123 W Ave N
Madison SD 57042

Call Sign: K0BSW
Robert C Schaaf
1009 W Center St
Madison SD 57042

Call Sign: W0CKT
W Edward Marquart
Madison SD 570420443

FCC Amateur Radio Licenses in Marion

Call Sign: KC0VYU
Dean F Tieszen
44633 274th St
Marion SD 570430178

Call Sign: N0UHL
Thomas J Ensz
304 Center St
Marion SD 57043

Call Sign: W0KXU
Vernon J Hofer
RR1
Marion SD 57043

FCC Amateur Radio Licenses in Martin

Call Sign: N3NTV
David W Vowell
901 4th Ave
Martin SD 57551

Call Sign: WA0PDE
Melvin R Leeper
203 Swallow
Martin SD 57551

Call Sign: N9UZW
Kim E Dewhurst
502 Swallow St Box 625
Martin SD 57551

Call Sign: K0BJM
Bernardine Ness
Blue Cloud Abbey
Marvin SD 57251

Call Sign: K0GDR
Basil O Dilger
Blue Cloud Abbey
Marvin SD 572510098

FCC Amateur Radio Licenses in McCook Lake

Call Sign: KC0FVR
Roy E Nickum
607 Lakeshore Dr
McCook Lake SD 570494008

Call Sign: K0ROY
Roy E Nickum
607 Lakeshore Dr
McCook Lake SD 570494008

Call Sign: KB0ZQE
Patrice A Kistner
603 Lakeshore Dr
McCook Lake SD 57049

Call Sign: KB2WZJ
Mary Burns A Verlaque
125 N Shore Dr
McCook Lake SD 57049

Call Sign: N0WHH
Thomas R Burns
125 N Shore Dr
McCook Lake SD 57049

Call Sign: KB2WZK
Christian G Verlaque
125 N Shore Dr
McCook Lake SD 57049

Call Sign: N1ERM
Julia S Heaton
65 Northshore Dr
McCook Lake SD 57049

Call Sign: N7VU
Timothy H Heaton
65 Northshore Dr
McCook Lake SD 57049

FCC Amateur Radio Licenses in McLaughlin

Call Sign: KA0MEI
Domenico Procida
302 1st Ave E
McLaughlin SD 57642

FCC Amateur Radio Licenses in Mellette

Call Sign: KA0HVL
Harold Stevens
Mellette SD 57461

FCC Amateur Radio Licenses in Menno

Call Sign: KJ0M
James W Schnaidt
Menno SD 57045

Call Sign: KA0HLO
Douglas C Schafer
Menno SD 57045

FCC Amateur Radio Licenses in Milbank

Call Sign: N0ILQ
James M Carlson
48364 151st St
Milbank SD 57252

Call Sign: KD0RHT
Mark L Loeschke
15524 485th Ave
Milbank SD 57252

Call Sign: N0RMR
Roger A Hoff
606 E 4th Ave
Milbank SD 57252

Call Sign: K0CKU
Darrel E Richards
204 Eastman 2
Milbank SD 57252

Call Sign: KB0AIM
William J Vissers
211 N Dakota St
Milbank SD 57252

Call Sign: N0YZH
John R Pahl
308 S 2nd St
Milbank SD 57252

Call Sign: KA0UEQ
James J Thomas
606 S 6th St
Milbank SD 57252

Call Sign: KB0AIL
William P Unker
311 S Viola
Milbank SD 57252

Call Sign: KC0MYW
Nick J Welder
1101 W Milbank Ave
Milbank SD 57252

Call Sign: KD0RDX
Jonathan D Rogers
111 W Park Ave
Milbank SD 57252

FCC Amateur Radio Licenses in Miller

Call Sign: KB0TTB
Karl O Engelmann
35731 208th St
Miller SD 573626811

Call Sign: KB0YPN
Dorothy A Engelmann
35731 208th St
Miller SD 573626811

Call Sign: KC0WNG
Douglas D Deboer
419 E 2nd Ave
Miller SD 57362

Call Sign: KB0LVR

Wayne M Nesby
320 E 2nd St
Miller SD 57362

Call Sign: KD0HI
Joe G Ruzicka
323 E 5th St
Miller SD 57362

Call Sign: WB0STS
Robert L Klages
603 E 7th St
Miller SD 57362

Call Sign: KA4CCK
Mildred E Richer
280 Mmaper Pl
Miller SD 57362

Call Sign: N0RQZ
Stephan D Schroeder
410 N Broadway
Miller SD 57362

FCC Amateur Radio Licenses in Mina

Call Sign: KC0QJZ
Thomas L Kessler
37160 133rd St
Mina SD 57451

Call Sign: WB0JZZ
Hub Amateur Radio Club
148 N Sunset Dr
Mina SD 57462

Call Sign: K0HAA
Jim W Rappe
148 N Sunset Dr
Mina SD 57451

Call Sign: KC0WPD
Rodney W Brandenburger
250 Nesbitt Dr
Mina SD 57451

FCC Amateur Radio Licenses in Mission

Call Sign: KB0HBP
William L Reese
Mission SD 57555

Call Sign: KD0IYJ
Caleb M Whiting
Mission SD 57555

FCC Amateur Radio Licenses in Mission Hill

Call Sign: N0QJN
James R Carlson
Rt 1
Mission Hill SD 57046

Call Sign: N0VC
Guy A Chaney
266 Wildwood Dr
Mission Hill SD 57045

FCC Amateur Radio Licenses in Mitchell

Call Sign: KB0RUN
Brian P Enga
40771 256th St
Mitchell SD 57301

Call Sign: KA0YJD
Lynn W Koerner
40447 260th St
Mitchell SD 57301

Call Sign: K0YNS
Keith A Bartels
25872 409th Ave
Mitchell SD 573015802

Call Sign: WD0FKB
David W Ver Steeg

1500 Augusta Ave
Mitchell SD 57301

Call Sign: WD0BRF
Kevin L Van Overschelde
209 E 10th
Mitchell SD 57301

Call Sign: WA0ORN
Leo L Van Overschelde
209 E 10th St
Mitchell SD 57301

Call Sign: KB0YPQ
Ralph G Roth
817 E 12th
Mitchell SD 57301

Call Sign: KB0OXO
Rodney W Weber
901 E 4th Ave
Mitchell SD 57301

Call Sign: KB0QXP
Allen L Gearey
320 E 5th
Mitchell SD 57301

Call Sign: KB0AAQ
Philip N Williams
920 E 5th
Mitchell SD 57301

Call Sign: KB0RHY
Lona S Gearey
320 E 5th Ave
Mitchell SD 57301

Call Sign: KB0YDW
Heather S Gearey
320 E 5th Ave
Mitchell SD 57301

Call Sign: KC0NQO
Rob E Moore

1030 E 5th Ave
Mitchell SD 57301

Call Sign: KA0PTN
Elmer Haugum
924 E 6th Ave
Mitchell SD 573012818

Call Sign: WB0MZB
Floyd A Eliason
1013 E 7th Ave
Mitchell SD 57301

Call Sign: WB0ZYO
Margaret H Eliason
1013 E 7th Ave
Mitchell SD 57301

Call Sign: W0ZSJ
Mitchell Amateur Radio Club
2525 E Havens
Mitchell SD 57301

Call Sign: N0MYE
John A Miedema
2525 E Havens St
Mitchell SD 57301

Call Sign: W0CLS
James E Blades
1416 Firesteel Dr
Mitchell SD 573012151

Call Sign: N0LCL
Brian J Kelly
40990 Mc Kinley Pl
Mitchell SD 57301

Call Sign: KB0DSG
Dean Knutson
701 N Blair St
Mitchell SD 57301

Call Sign: WB0AUK
Richard L Stedman

1201 N Capital
Mitchell SD 57301

209 W 10th
Mitchell SD 57301

Call Sign: WA0SDL
Marvin E Pooley
805 N Duff St
Mitchell SD 57301

Call Sign: KB0ORV
Howard J Gorter
600 W 15th Ave Apt 14
Mitchell SD 57301

Call Sign: W0GKE
Ronald D Gates Sr
113 N Harmon Dr
Mitchell SD 57301

Call Sign: KB0ZCD
Lindy S Graves
420 W 19th Ave 10
Mitchell SD 57301

Call Sign: KA0PTM
Willard A Payne
1414 N Langdon
Mitchell SD 57301

Call Sign: KB0NBK
Tony D Russell
1120 W 4th Ave
Mitchell SD 57301

Call Sign: WD5DQW
Donald W Montgomery
1547 N Ridge Rd
Mitchell SD 573011540

Call Sign: K4NW
Mike B Murdock
700 W 7th Ave
Mitchell SD 57301

Call Sign: N0RAM
David J Rohan
700 S Davison St
Mitchell SD 57301

Call Sign: KG4PRI
Abbe H Murdock
700 W 7th Ave
Mitchell SD 57301

Call Sign: KC0RWY
Micaela E Nelson
500 S Minnesota
Mitchell SD 57301

Call Sign: KB0QXY
William F Peacock
1000 W Hanson
Mitchell SD 57103

Call Sign: WA0KEM
Dwight J Pooley
211 S Montana St
Mitchell SD 57301

Call Sign: KC0MLO
William F Peacock
1000 W Hanson
Mitchell SD 57103

Call Sign: W0GWW
Lawrence J Webb
705 S Rowley
Mitchell SD 57301

Call Sign: N0ARU
William F Peacock
1000 W Hanson St
Mitchell SD 57301

Call Sign: W0GWL
Paul P Kowall

Call Sign: WB0OMD
Grace E Boisen

725 W Norway Ave
Mitchell SD 57301

Call Sign: KB0UZJ
Kevin C Manke
1104 Woods Cir
Mitchell SD 57301

Call Sign: KC0VFW
Joseph C Manke
1104 Woods Cir
Mitchell SD 57301

Call Sign: WA0SIJ
Melvin D Pooley
Mitchell SD 57301

FCC Amateur Radio Licenses in Mobridge

Call Sign: KB0ONC
Douglas W Westerlund
210 10th St E
Mobridge SD 57601

Call Sign: KC7RJZ
Dennis W Swofford
807 1st Ave E
Mobridge SD 57601

Call Sign: WA0MRY
Frank A Kraft
808 1st Ave W
Mobridge SD 576012113

Call Sign: NY0X
Leland L Keszler
810 1st Ave W
Mobridge SD 57601

Call Sign: KA0LOV
Edward B Ries
814 2nd Ave E
Mobridge SD 57601

Call Sign: K0ERM
Fred D Dekker
617 2nd Ave W
Mobridge SD 57601

Call Sign: KA0HMH
Helen N Cory
815 2nd Ave W
Mobridge SD 57601

Call Sign: W0YMB
Roland L Cory
815 2nd Ave W
Mobridge SD 57601

Call Sign: KA0VDK
Duane D Delzer
608 4th Ave E
Mobridge SD 57601

Call Sign: KA0VDL
Clayton D Delzer
902 E 1st Ave
Mobridge SD 576011801

Call Sign: KA0UDE
Douglas C Nelson
1605 Pondarosa Ave
Mobridge SD 57601

Call Sign: N0XOG
Ronald C Pringle
1203 W 3rd Ave
Mobridge SD 57601

Call Sign: KA8RVL
Arthur H Brown III
717 W 9th Ave
Mobridge SD 57601

FCC Amateur Radio Licenses in Monroe

Call Sign: W0OJY
Prairie Dog Amateur Radio Club

127 Ash St
Monroe SD 57047

Call Sign: WB0VBW
John L Nesladek
127 W Ash St
Monroe SD 57047

FCC Amateur Radio Licenses in Montrose

Call Sign: KB0ACO
Dean B Ruedebusch
45007 SD Hwy 38
Montrose SD 570485719

FCC Amateur Radio Licenses in Mound City

Call Sign: KC0HWP
Kevin L Ackerman
RR1
Mound City SD 57646

FCC Amateur Radio Licenses in Mount Vernon

Call Sign: W0SDP
Albert A Scott Sr
24431 393 Ave
Mount Vernon SD 573635501

Call Sign: WB0HBL
James A Johnson
24628 394th Ave
Mount Vernon SD 57363

Call Sign: WB0OME
Joan L Johnson
24628 394th Ave
Mount Vernon SD 57363

Call Sign: WB0RSB
Albert L Schulz
25202 398th Ave

Mount Vernon SD 57363

Call Sign: KD0JJH
Loren D Brech
307 N Lindman
Mount Vernon SD 57363

Call Sign: KB0QBT
Doug E Backer
203 N Main
Mount Vernon SD 57363

Call Sign: AA0AK
Paul D Morris
401 W 3rd St
Mount Vernon SD 57363

Call Sign: WB0EPY
John R Boisen
Mount Vernon SD 57363

FCC Amateur Radio Licenses in Murdo

Call Sign: W0TAS
Carrol A Andrews
605 Garfield Ave
Murdo SD 57559

Call Sign: KB0WMZ
Karen J Hoekman
122 Main St
Murdo SD 57559

Call Sign: KB0WMY
Karl W Hoekman
122 N Main
Murdo SD 57559

FCC Amateur Radio Licenses in New Effington

Call Sign: W0MDD
John B Ohnstad
RR1

New Effington SD 572559744

Call Sign: KB9YVH
John M Paul
60 Whittier Ave
New Effington SD 57255

FCC Amateur Radio Licenses in New Underwood

Call Sign: KA1OTT
Anthony B Ascrizzi
505 S B Ave
New Underwood SD 577610231

Call Sign: KB0WCE
Joyce E Jeffries
New Underwood SD 577610184

Call Sign: KC0KXW
Marc W Myers
New Underwood SD 577610091

Call Sign: KC0KXX
Jacqueline H Myers
New Underwood SD 577610091

Call Sign: N0GMP
David R Jeffries
New Underwood SD 577610184

Call Sign: AA7JJ
Gordon D Standart
New Underwood SD 577610344

FCC Amateur Radio Licenses in Newell

Call Sign: KD0GRF
Steven K Goff
13820 Lewis Rd
Newell SD 57760

Call Sign: N1BUI
Stephanie D Snowden

RR1
Newell SD 57760

Call Sign: WY7WY
Charles H Larsen
102 S Dartmouth Ave
Newell SD 57760

FCC Amateur Radio Licenses in Nisland

Call Sign: K0VVX
Carl L Bruce
601 2nd St
Nisland SD 57762

FCC Amateur Radio Licenses in North Sioux City

Call Sign: WD5CYP
Philip T Dickinson
101 Cotts Dr Lot 84
North Sioux City SD 57049

Call Sign: WD0ETH
Dennis D Mortensen
250 Courtyard Dr Apt 209
North Sioux City SD 57049

Call Sign: KD0MKD
Julia S Heaton
65 Northshore Dr
North Sioux City SD 57049

Call Sign: N1ERM
Julia S Heaton
65 Northshore Dr
North Sioux City SD 57049

Call Sign: KB0AUY
Nickolas Johnson
Rv Park Lot 10
North Sioux City SD 57049

Call Sign: N0OTJ

Scott R Nurnberg
657 St er Dr Apt 506
North Sioux City SD 57049

Call Sign: KA0ZEZ
Kyle W Kruse
North Sioux City SD 57049

FCC Amateur Radio Licenses in Northville

Call Sign: KC0WTI
Alice M Irvine
Northville SD 57465

Call Sign: KA0FLL
Alice M Irvine
Northville SD 57465

FCC Amateur Radio Licenses in Oacoma

Call Sign: N0WRO
Diana R Goos
Oacoma SD 57365

FCC Amateur Radio Licenses in Oelrichs

Call Sign: KD0DZG
Ronald L Trent
13924 Lennon School Rd
Oelrichs SD 57763

Call Sign: W0RLT
Ronald L Trent
13924 Lennon School Rd
Oelrichs SD 57763

Call Sign: KD0GTD
Larry J Osmotherly
13871 Old Hwy 79
Oelrichs SD 57763

Call Sign: N0YJF

Maynard D Britain
Oelrichs SD 57763

Call Sign: AB0MN
John E Davies
Oelrichs SD 57763

Call Sign: KD0GTE
Heath W Greenough
Oelrichs SD 57763

FCC Amateur Radio Licenses in Onida

Call Sign: KB0SBU
Todd K Glanzer
17951 300th Ave
Onida SD 57564

Call Sign: KI5CT
Lavern M Patrick
600 S 8th St
Onida SD 57564

Call Sign: KB0MJD
Douglas G Marsh
Onida SD 57564

FCC Amateur Radio Licenses in Oral

Call Sign: KA0FNF
Dewayne E Connell
Oral SD 57766

FCC Amateur Radio Licenses in Parker

Call Sign: W7XU
Arliss N Thompson
45720 268th St
Parker SD 57053

Call Sign: KC0LHQ
Nolan N C Thompson
45720 268th St

Parker SD 57053

Call Sign: N0LAN
Nolan N C Thompson
45720 268th St
Parker SD 57053

Call Sign: N0QJM
Holly C Thompson
45720 268th St
Parker SD 57053

Call Sign: N0SPZ
Edwin L Smith
44822 279th St
Parker SD 57053

Call Sign: KB0SJJ
Jeffery E Roberts
217 Poplar
Parker SD 57053

FCC Amateur Radio Licenses in Parkston

Call Sign: KB0HAI
Anthony J Heck
23714 411th Ave
Parkston SD 57366

FCC Amateur Radio Licenses in Parmelee

Call Sign: KA0HZI
Edna Nisly
5713 S Herren Rd
Parmelee SD 57566

FCC Amateur Radio Licenses in Peever

Call Sign: KA0HMI
Delton R Gerber
RR1
Peever SD 57257

FCC Amateur Radio Licenses in Philip

Call Sign: N0ERA
Harry W Schofield
203 SW Ave
Philip SD 57567

Call Sign: KC0DH
Bette L Lawler
Philip SD 57567

Call Sign: K0BMS
Bette L Lawler
Philip SD 57567

FCC Amateur Radio Licenses in Piedmont

Call Sign: W0DAK
Chapter 102 Qcwa
15362 Canyon Trail
Piedmont SD 57769

Call Sign: WA0VKC
Scott E Rausch
15362 Canyon Trail
Piedmont SD 57769

Call Sign: KD0ETG
Prairie Rovers Amateur Radio Club
15362 Canyon Trail
Piedmont SD 577697286

Call Sign: W0JR
Prairie Rovers Amateur Radio Club
15362 Canyon Trail
Piedmont SD 577697286

Call Sign: KC0RMQ
Rick E Guth
12681 Erickson Ranch Rd
Piedmont SD 57769

Call Sign: KA0IKA
Gordon W Quam
HC 80
Piedmont SD 57769

Call Sign: W3IKT
Glen L Fiala
11901 Lofty Pines Rd
Piedmont SD 57769

Call Sign: N0AXR
Fred A Brown
Piedmont Rt Box 451
Piedmont SD 57769

Call Sign: KA0GIF
Mary E Kottwitz
Piedmont SD 57769

Call Sign: KC0ETE
Victor J Kottwitz
Piedmont SD 577690145

Call Sign: N0BOH
Jeffery R Kottwitz
Piedmont SD 577690145

Call Sign: K0YDM
Wayne J Schmidt
Pierpont SD 57468

FCC Amateur Radio Licenses in Pierre

Call Sign: KC0WIF
Paul Lee
126 Blue Jay Rd
Pierre SD 57501

Call Sign: AA0LY
Tamrid T Gatje
3660 Bond Pl
Pierre SD 57501

Call Sign: KB0SEY

Pierre Amateur Radio Club
3660 Bond Pl
Pierre SD 57501

Call Sign: W0PIR
Pierre Amateur Radio Club
3660 Bond Pl
Pierre SD 57501

Call Sign: KB8OZR
Charlotte A Hersman
7155 Buchanan
Pierre SD 57501

Call Sign: N0NPO
Gregory S Bond
2829 Buhl Ave
Pierre SD 575016327

Call Sign: KB0MJB
Seth A Graves
105 Capital Hill Dr
Pierre SD 57501

Call Sign: N0QGW
James P Graham
1101 Corral Rd
Pierre SD 57501

Call Sign: KE4SDQ
Robert E Bogart
1203 E Broadway Ave
Pierre SD 575013435

Call Sign: WB0RJH
Gregory C Hall
1312 E Cabot St
Pierre SD 575013408

Call Sign: KB0PGV
Odean Solberg
1900 E Capitol Ave
Pierre SD 57501

Call Sign: WB9MWH

Timothy J Lors
1027 E Dakota
Pierre SD 57501

Call Sign: KB0MJC
Dean A Wallace
1210 E Missouri
Pierre SD 57501

Call Sign: KC0WVG
Sara R Anderson
2107 E Park
Pierre SD 57501

Call Sign: N0YZJ
Kenneth E Roberts
2415 E Park St
Pierre SD 57501

Call Sign: KD0MHW
Chris M Boxley
2515 E Sally
Pierre SD 57501

Call Sign: KC0BTQ
Bruce A Olson
2218 E Sully
Pierre SD 57501

Call Sign: KC0AYI
Bonnie J Bauder
2603 E Sully
Pierre SD 57501

Call Sign: KB0BWW
Bobby L Van Winsen
2310 E Sully Ave
Pierre SD 57501

Call Sign: N0MWK
Michael K Smith
113 Eagle Dr
Pierre SD 57501

Call Sign: KB0SBB

Gary N Whitney
1301 Edgewater Dr
Pierre SD 575011345

Call Sign: K0YXD
Julayne A Brude
1300 Edgewater Dr 402
Pierre SD 57501

Call Sign: N0GJX
Ronald E Wham
1615 Grandview St
Pierre SD 57501

Call Sign: WB0BDY
Peggy L Hyde
19730 Grey Goose Rd
Pierre SD 57501

Call Sign: N0OMR
Jay M Etzkorn
HC 31
Pierre SD 57501

Call Sign: N0YFF
Matt D King
HC 31
Pierre SD 57501

Call Sign: W0RTD
Eldon L Lindquist
29680 Hwy 34 E
Pierre SD 57501

Call Sign: WB0LLQ
Betty A Lindquist
29680 Hwy 34 E
Pierre SD 57501

Call Sign: KC0BUG
Neils M Christoffersen
2020 Kennedy Dr
Pierre SD 57501

Call Sign: KB0OUJ

James L Hammond
29640 Lakeview Pl
Pierre SD 57501

Call Sign: KC0EFX
Wesley A Hiller
1005 Marina Ave
Pierre SD 57501

Call Sign: N0RRA
William C Kelley
126 N Adams Ave
Pierre SD 57501

Call Sign: N0MDS
Jonathan M Mahorney
316 N Buchanan
Pierre SD 57501

Call Sign: KC0ODP
Paul W Sheldon
1021 N Central Ave
Pierre SD 57501

Call Sign: KC0OCI
Scott D Sheldon
1021 N Central Ave
Pierre SD 57501

Call Sign: KE7DEL
Neil L Padgett
711 N Grand Ave
Pierre SD 57501

Call Sign: KC0CHJ
Richard L Donahue
106 N Harrison Ave
Pierre SD 57501

Call Sign: K0PIR
Richard L Donahue
106 N Harrison Ave
Pierre SD 57501

Call Sign: KG0GD

Scott A Nelson
639 N Highland 16
Pierre SD 57501

Call Sign: KC0CHG
Myra J Christensen
503 N Jackson
Pierre SD 575012622

Call Sign: KC0CHI
Mark C Gildemaster
307 N Johnson Ave
Pierre SD 57501

Call Sign: KC0AYH
Jed A Hillestad
612 N Oneida
Pierre SD 57501

Call Sign: KB0KNJ
Dale P Healey
524 N Oneida Ave
Pierre SD 57501

Call Sign: W0KPV
Comet W Haraldson
108 N Pierce
Pierre SD 57501

Call Sign: KF8HW
Lawrence D Sluiter
200 N Pierce Ave
Pierre SD 57501

Call Sign: KB0SBD
Robert M Wallace
224 N Poplar
Pierre SD 57501

Call Sign: W7GKZ
Robert F Benson
207 N Tyler
Pierre SD 57501

Call Sign: WB0NNI

Robert L Hopper
125 Norbeck
Pierre SD 57501

Call Sign: KC0YCB
Laura R Hopper
125 Norbeck Dr
Pierre SD 57501

Call Sign: WB0RWH
Robert W Hopper
125 Norbeck Dr
Pierre SD 57501

Call Sign: KI4NEA
Zeke K Saukel
120 Orion Ave
Pierre SD 57501

Call Sign: KB0GGM
Randall L Anderson
2921 Oxford Ct
Pierre SD 57501

Call Sign: N0RQY
Vickee R Anderson
2921 Oxford Ct
Pierre SD 57501

Call Sign: K0SDA
Gregory J Adams
17831 Quantum Pl
Pierre SD 57501

Call Sign: KF0FN
James D Zahradnicek
20310 Redwood Pl
Pierre SD 57501

Call Sign: KC0CHH
Donald R Hayward
20315 Redwood Pl
Pierre SD 575016310

Call Sign: WB0QVE

Jodene J Rausch
104 River View Dr
Pierre SD 57501

Call Sign: N0UJH
George E Teige
914 S Arthur
Pierre SD 57501

Call Sign: N7JVQ
Virgil L Minden Jr
1111 S Cleveland Ave
Pierre SD 57501

Call Sign: W0GZU
Ty Rensch
112 S Court Pl
Pierre SD 575013301

Call Sign: KB0GBS
James E Marsh
1005 S Garfield
Pierre SD 57501

Call Sign: N0UJG
Ronald A Smith
428 S Lincoln
Pierre SD 57501

Call Sign: AA0TS
Jeffrey S Kelley
330 S Polk
Pierre SD 57501

Call Sign: KB0MJE
Daniel S Kelley
330 S Polk
Pierre SD 57501

Call Sign: N0VFS
Shari L Zahradnicek
29563 SD Hwy 14 83
Pierre SD 57501

Call Sign: KC0OCH

Karen M Zahradnicek
29563 SD Hwy 14 83
Pierre SD 57501

Call Sign: KC0FBL
Matt P Hicks
2200 SD Hwy 1804
Pierre SD 57501

Call Sign: KB0PZX
Laurel G Selken
216 Sunshine Loop
Pierre SD 57501

Call Sign: N0WTG
Gale N Selken
216 Sunshine Loop
Pierre SD 57501

Call Sign: KF0OM
Donald M Armstrong
2751 Sussex Rd
Pierre SD 575015635

Call Sign: KD0S
James D Zahradnicek
29563 US Hwy 14
Pierre SD 57501

Call Sign: WD0T
Todd R Dravland
29567 US Hwy 14
Pierre SD 57501

Call Sign: N0IBX
Wyman A Whitney
400 W 2nd St
Pierre SD 57501

Call Sign: N0OMP
Edward L Wallace
621 W 2nd St
Pierre SD 57501

Call Sign: KC0GUF

Robert W Hopper
620 W Prospect
Pierre SD 57501

Call Sign: KB0PGX
Tony J Ondricek
721 Wells Ave Apt 19
Pierre SD 57501

Call Sign: KD0DRQ
Darin P Bergquist
1100 Westwood Dr
Pierre SD 57501

Call Sign: K0IE
Darin P Bergquist
1100 Westwood Dr
Pierre SD 57501

Call Sign: KB0FBK
Howard L Grinager
904 Winchester Dr
Pierre SD 57501

Call Sign: AA0HV
Elton M Henderson
Pierre SD 57501

Call Sign: N0PIZ
John Opp
Pierre SD 57501

Call Sign: WB0NET
Blaine C Olson
Pierre SD 57501

Call Sign: W0CQN
Harley M Wallace
Pierre SD 57501

Call Sign: AA0CT
Gary E Wallace
Pierre SD 57501

Call Sign: KC0WVF

James M Ward
Pierre SD 575010135

FCC Amateur Radio Licenses in Pine Ridge

Call Sign: KI0OZ
William A Schnurr
Hospital Housing Compound
Pine Ridge SD 577703018

Call Sign: KB0ZVR
Laura V Graham
Pine Ridge SD 57770

Call Sign: KC0FOM
Julie K Dixon
Pine Ridge SD 57770

FCC Amateur Radio Licenses in Plankinton

Call Sign: N0KAW
Paul D Schneider
602 E State St
Plankinton SD 57368

Call Sign: WB0EKL
Jesse S Johnson
RR1
Plankinton SD 57368

FCC Amateur Radio Licenses in Platte

Call Sign: K0GF
George W Fish Jr
36044 277th St
Platte SD 57369

Call Sign: KA7QHQ
Jimmy R Christopherson
28222 361st Ave
Platte SD 57369

Call Sign: KC7DUI
Charles H Aurand III
500 E 1st St
Platte SD 57369

Call Sign: KC0LDM
Charles H Aurand III
500 E 1st St
Platte SD 57369

Call Sign: AB0RV
Charles H Aurand III
500 E 1st St
Platte SD 57369

Call Sign: WB0OMF
Helen S Gray
601 E 7th Box 200
Platte SD 57369

Call Sign: N0XDT
James K Soesbe
Platte SD 57369

FCC Amateur Radio Licenses in Pollock

Call Sign: N3WQD
Dennis G Dockter
Pollock SD 57648

Call Sign: N3XAE
Beth A Dockter
Pollock SD 57648

Call Sign: N3XQZ
Tabitha R Dockter
Pollock SD 57648

FCC Amateur Radio Licenses in Pringle

Call Sign: KC0OO
Fredric J Stephan
Wind Cave Ranch

Pringle SD 57773

FCC Amateur Radio Licenses in Rapid City

Call Sign: KB0OHN
Randall E Cain
709 12th St
Rapid City SD 57701

Call Sign: AA0HK
Robert L Mc Ginnis
1010 13 E St Patrick
Rapid City SD 57707

Call Sign: WD0CBP
William L Reynolds
239 38th St
Rapid City SD 577022102

Call Sign: WA0CIP
Joseph H Abeln
2009 5th St
Rapid City SD 57701

Call Sign: KC0SFA
Jessica J Duba
1922 6th St
Rapid City SD 57701

Call Sign: W0NBX
Danny L Richmond
2419 Alamo Dr
Rapid City SD 577025123

Call Sign: W0XH
Harvey L Sachau
9 Anaconda Rd
Rapid City SD 57701

Call Sign: WB0ZBX
Linda J Sachau
9 Anaconda Rd
Rapid City SD 57701

Call Sign: WA0YFO
Gerald J Heckel
110 Anaconda Rd
Rapid City SD 57701

Call Sign: WB0LSQ
Everett W Holmgrain
23756 Arena Dr
Rapid City SD 57702

Call Sign: KI0SU
Everett W Holmgrain
23756 Arena Dr
Rapid City SD 57702

Call Sign: WB0LSQ
Everett W Holmgrain
23756 Arena Dr
Rapid City SD 57702

Call Sign: KC0QPW
W Vail Williams
23756 Arena Dr
Rapid City SD 57702

Call Sign: KD0MZ
William M Whitenton
23756 Arena Dr 13606
Rapid City SD 57702

Call Sign: KD0ETF
Donald L Robertson
23756 Arena Dr 14792
Rapid City SD 57702

Call Sign: N0DLM
Donald L Robertson
23756 Arena Dr 14792
Rapid City SD 57702

Call Sign: N0MRC
Steven H Kerkhoff
23756 Arena Dr 18338
Rapid City SD 57702

Call Sign: KA0OHI
Jerl E Pringle
3620 Arizona
Rapid City SD 57701

Call Sign: KB0YJQ
James M Murphree
2301 Arrow St
Rapid City SD 57702

Call Sign: K0UDZ
Eugene M Wasson
4555 Ashland Rd
Rapid City SD 577018552

Call Sign: KB0CJO
Tycho D Castberg
1320 Atlas St 5 302
Rapid City SD 57701

Call Sign: KB1DWN
Shashi Kanth
5594 Barberry Cir
Rapid City SD 57702

Call Sign: N0BKX
Alex J De Mersseman
329 Basham Rd
Rapid City SD 57702

Call Sign: KB0UGU
Jason R Erickson
717 Belmont Dr
Rapid City SD 57702

Call Sign: WA0FPR
Robert J Olson
6524 Beverly Dr Weston Hgt
Rapid City SD 57701

Call Sign: KA0PYT
Sheryl J Bauer
713 Blaine
Rapid City SD 57701

Call Sign: KX0U
Gene F Bauer
713 Blaine Ave
Rapid City SD 57701

Call Sign: KB0HUP
Curtiss A Sween
10569 Briarwood Ct
Rapid City SD 57702

Call Sign: K0CXB
O Dale Sayler
3333 Broadmoor Dr
Rapid City SD 57702

Call Sign: W0AGG
William B Porter
4226 Brookside Dr
Rapid City SD 577022030

Call Sign: K0RSS
Russell E Skinner
4322 Brookside Dr
Rapid City SD 57702

Call Sign: N0YOL
Robert J Ewing
3916 Brookside Dr
Rapid City SD 57702

Call Sign: N0MND
Dennis W Williams
22376 Bunco Ct
Rapid City SD 57701

Call Sign: KD0DLC
Brian D Killion
22989 Candlelight Dr
Rapid City SD 57703

Call Sign: WB0VKM
Michael L Steed
4503 Candlewood Pl 103
Rapid City SD 57702

Call Sign: KC0ZQD
Neal J Richmond
4405 Candlewood Pl 206
Rapid City SD 57702

Call Sign: KD0GYK
Karl D Diekevers
4526 Candlewood Pl 306
Rapid City SD 57702

Call Sign: KC0VZV
James J Doyle
6701 Carnoustie Ct
Rapid City SD 57702

Call Sign: KA0PRE
Kara L Sewell
2010 Cedar Dr
Rapid City SD 57701

Call Sign: KB0ZSW
Karen S Woods
4716 Chalkstone Dr
Rapid City SD 57701

Call Sign: N0NAC
James C Woods Jr
4716 Chalkstone Dr
Rapid City SD 57701

Call Sign: KC0EAC
Angela L Monheim
411 City Springs Ln
Rapid City SD 577020147

Call Sign: KB0WRU
Christine Elyse K Gunderson
1210 Clover Ridge Ct
Rapid City SD 57701

Call Sign: KC0VZO
Logan A Loeb
4011 Clover St
Rapid City SD 57702

Call Sign: AC0LU
Logan A Loeb
4011 Clover St
Rapid City SD 57702

Call Sign: KF0XO
Norbert A Sichterman
4425 Colt Ln
Rapid City SD 57701

Call Sign: N0ZZQ
Harry B Brist
1608 Copperdale Dr
Rapid City SD 57703

Call Sign: KC0DHS
Jerry L Fincher Jr
1403 Copperfiel Dr
Rapid City SD 577034742

Call Sign: KE4MJG
William H Dart
3021 Copperlane Ct
Rapid City SD 57703

Call Sign: N0APE
Howard L Homan
14667 Cordes Ln
Rapid City SD 57701

Call Sign: N0EEH
Irvin W Cannon
3375 Corral Dr
Rapid City SD 57702

Call Sign: KC0MMQ
Tonya R Taggart
3421 Cottonwood Apt 3
Rapid City SD 57702

Call Sign: KF0AM
Robert L Henriksen
14693 Country Rd
Rapid City SD 57701

Call Sign: N0ZHV
Earl R Voeller
1980 Country Rd 47
Rapid City SD 57701

Call Sign: KB0MWN
Adam R Trobee
1980 Country Rd 79
Rapid City SD 57701

Call Sign: KD0YH
Lavern L Haas
8299 Countryside Blvd
Rapid City SD 57702

Call Sign: N0ANI
Lawrence R Palmer
2051 Covington St
Rapid City SD 57701

Call Sign: N0UKO
Charles R Palmer
2051 Covington St
Rapid City SD 577036344

Call Sign: N0UKP
Frances A Palmer
2051 Covington St
Rapid City SD 577036344

Call Sign: AC0WT
Kenneth R Broomfield
631 Crestview Dr
Rapid City SD 57702

Call Sign: KD7NII
Jason W Warr
7550 Crossbill Cir
Rapid City SD 57702

Call Sign: W0DBA
Jason W Warr
7550 Crossbill Cir
Rapid City SD 57702

Call Sign: KA0NYU
Dana R Parker
7808 Croyle Ave
Rapid City SD 57702

Call Sign: K0QLO
Howard D Roberson
8003 Croyle Ave
Rapid City SD 57702

Call Sign: WA0WVW
Jacobus P C Van Der Geest
2102 Cruz
Rapid City SD 57702

Call Sign: KC0RTV
Edward S Cromwell
2313 Cruz Dr
Rapid City SD 57702

Call Sign: WD0EMQ
John E Tipton
246 Curtis St
Rapid City SD 57701

Call Sign: KD0OYB
Michelle N Taylor
15350 Dawkins Rd
Rapid City SD 57703

Call Sign: AL7BY
Gene H Deck
1617 Debra Dr 101
Rapid City SD 577021012

Call Sign: KC0VZS
Alex L Calderon
1617 Debra Dr 404
Rapid City SD 57702

Call Sign: AA0YZ
David A Torgenrud
110 Denver St Apt 110
Rapid City SD 57701

Call Sign: KD0CZX
Daniel J Linole
4141 Derby Ln
Rapid City SD 57701

Call Sign: KB0ZNF
Alf Kare E Riisnaes
3410 Dover St
Rapid City SD 57702

Call Sign: KB0ZNG
Catherine L Riisnaes
3410 Dover St
Rapid City SD 57702

Call Sign: K0ARE
Alf Kare E Riisnaes
3410 Dover St
Rapid City SD 57702

Call Sign: K0CTY
Catherine Riisnaes
3410 Dover St
Rapid City SD 57702

Call Sign: KB0WI
Paul M Michael
8532 Dunsmore Rd
Rapid City SD 57702

Call Sign: N0QWX
Ronald L Mc Mullen
8562 Dunsmore Rd
Rapid City SD 577028972

Call Sign: KD0JLR
Brady A Begeman
717 E Anamosa St Apt 107
Rapid City SD 57701

Call Sign: N0DKV
Thomas P Brewer
743 E Anamosa St Bldg 3 Apt 105
Rapid City SD 57701

Call Sign: WA0MFZ
Harry A Martens
122 E Centennial St
Rapid City SD 57701

Call Sign: KD0CZZ
Judith L Martens
122 E Centennial St
Rapid City SD 57701

Call Sign: WA0TXG
Judith L Martens
122 E Centennial St
Rapid City SD 57701

Call Sign: KC0ST
John C Thomason
217 E College St
Rapid City SD 577011031

Call Sign: N0HCP
Daniel J Nagel
213 E Custer
Rapid City SD 57701

Call Sign: KD7PPA
Susan I Gasper
434 E Fairmont Blvd Apt 30
Rapid City SD 57701

Call Sign: WM1F
Mark C Wilson
3570 E Hwy 44
Rapid City SD 577036057

Call Sign: W0NIW
Francis A Hodgin
806 E Iowa St
Rapid City SD 57701

Call Sign: N6LTT
Curtis L Muehl
311 E Madison
Rapid City SD 57701

Call Sign: KF4NTG
Michael J Stanley
108 E Madison St
Rapid City SD 57701

Call Sign: KD0EWU
Peter J Stapley
715 E Minnesota 304
Rapid City SD 57701

Call Sign: N0SWO
Steve W Johnson
502 E Oakland
Rapid City SD 57701

Call Sign: K0BJF
Barbara J Fuller
1112 E Oakland St
Rapid City SD 577015857

Call Sign: N0MN
Richard L Fuller
1112 E Oakland St
Rapid City SD 577015857

Call Sign: KD0NAN
Korey Kelly
1301 E Oakland St Unit A
Rapid City SD 57701

Call Sign: KB0JPQ
Marc P Melucas
713 E Ohio St
Rapid City SD 57701

Call Sign: W0PUF
Alan C Bergman
909 E Ohio St
Rapid City SD 57701

Call Sign: KD0DAA
David J Huft
501 E Saint Joseph Rh 297
Rapid City SD 57701

Call Sign: KC0FCH
Chris J Hofer
501 E Saint Joseph St
Rapid City SD 577016017

Call Sign: KD0RAS
Christopher J Jaques
501 E Saint Joseph St
Rapid City SD 57701

Call Sign: KC0MMT
Josh T Millard
501 E Saint Joseph St
Rapid City SD 57704

Call Sign: K0VVY
South Dakota School Of Mines &
Technology Arc
501 E Saint Joseph St
Rapid City SD 577013995

Call Sign: KC0VIR
Rapid City Nws Amateur Radio Club
300 E Signal Dr
Rapid City SD 577013800

Call Sign: WX0UNR
Rapid City Nws Amateur Radio Club
300 E Signal Dr
Rapid City SD 577013800

Call Sign: KD0JLW
Maxwell J Sparks
501 E St Joseph SR 645
Rapid City SD 57701

Call Sign: KC0RTT
Ryan C Mckean
501 E St Joseph St
Rapid City SD 57701

Call Sign: KC0MMS
Brian P Vander Lugt
501 E St Joseph St P321
Rapid City SD 57701

Call Sign: W2FI
Floyd S Irons
1010 E St Patrick St Lot 21
Rapid City SD 57701

Call Sign: KB0WYB
Kimberly S Pierce
130 Fairmont Blvd
Rapid City SD 57701

Call Sign: NU0F
Frank R Shaw
118 E Van Buren
Rapid City SD 57701

Call Sign: AB0ML
Kimberly P Bagby
130 Fairmont Blvd
Rapid City SD 57701

Call Sign: KD0NJK
Edwin J Hickenbotham
511 E Van Buren St
Rapid City SD 57701

Call Sign: N0QI
Kimberly P Bagby
130 Fairmont Blvd
Rapid City SD 57701

Call Sign: KA0ZWL
Donald O Neff
4007 Elm Ave Apt 102
Rapid City SD 577018618

Call Sign: KC0EAA
Karen E Tallent
149 Fairmont Blvd
Rapid City SD 577017300

Call Sign: KC0TXU
Douglas V Aldrich
4907 Elmer St
Rapid City SD 57703

Call Sign: WB0PYM
William A Merchen
161 Fairmont Blvd
Rapid City SD 57701

Call Sign: W0SEB
Walter K Kjar
208 Enchantment Rd
Rapid City SD 57701

Call Sign: WB0QPM
Jane M Merchen
161 Fairmont Blvd
Rapid City SD 57701

Call Sign: KB0VBB
Daniel G Hern Jr
530 Ennen Dr
Rapid City SD 57701

Call Sign: KB6SRE
Cathleen L Hudgens
621 Fairmont Pl
Rapid City SD 57701

Call Sign: KC6PFD
Virgil L Stockstad
1110 Ennen Dr
Rapid City SD 57701

Call Sign: KB0UYJ
Randy M Bagby
130 Fairmont Rd
Rapid City SD 577015400

Call Sign: KD0RAQ
Steven J Lawler
7502 Erickson Ranch Rd
Rapid City SD 57702

Call Sign: AB0QY
Randy M Bagby
130 Fairmont Rd
Rapid City SD 577015400

Call Sign: K0RMB
Randy M Bagby
130 Fairmont Rd
Rapid City SD 577015400

Call Sign: N8WXS
Jeffrey L Campbell
3319 Flint Dr
Rapid City SD 57702

Call Sign: KB0WXZ
Tyler M Earnest
222 Flormann St
Rapid City SD 57701

Call Sign: KD0DKZ
Tracy A Perdue
4401 Forest Park Court
Rapid City SD 57702

Call Sign: KD0CQZ
Richard G Perdue
4401 Forest Park Ct
Rapid City SD 57702

Call Sign: KB0ISV
Bobby J Holder Sr
22880 Forest Rd
Rapid City SD 57702

Call Sign: N0XJF
Ashok V Kumar
616 Fox Run Dr
Rapid City SD 57701

Call Sign: WA0SXN
William G Huggins
821 Fox Run Dr 121
Rapid City SD 57701

Call Sign: W0QP
Donald B Tyson
821 Fox Run Dr 315
Rapid City SD 57701

Call Sign: KB0BXI
Leo P Griffin
821 Fox Run Dr Apt 214
Rapid City SD 577012376

Call Sign: KB0WYA
Louis J Simons
3614 Fraley Ct
Rapid City SD 57701

Call Sign: KC0BVL
Justin A England
907 Fulton St
Rapid City SD 57701

Call Sign: KD0KUZ
Michael A Heitland II
1929 Galaxy Dr
Rapid City SD 57701

Call Sign: KF4TR
Andre V Knott
3509 Gallery Ln
Rapid City SD 57702

Call Sign: W0IWE
Donald S Barnes
4944 Glenn St
Rapid City SD 57701

Call Sign: WD0HFK
Scot A Dannenbring
6879 Green Valley Dr
Rapid City SD 57701

Call Sign: KB0LSC
Marlene L Dannenbring
6879 Green Valley Dr
Rapid City SD 57703

Call Sign: WA0SD
Scot A Dannenbring
6879 Green Valley Dr
Rapid City SD 57703

Call Sign: KC0JYS
Scot E Dannenbring
6879 Green Valley Dr
Rapid City SD 57703

Call Sign: KC0JDR
Juanita L Clark
6731 Greenfield Dr
Rapid City SD 57703

Call Sign: KF4IBH
Jeremy J Garrow
6979 Greenfield Dr
Rapid City SD 57703

Call Sign: W0OPS
William L Hughes
6118 Greenleaf Ct
Rapid City SD 57702

Call Sign: KD0RAT
Christopher A Redmond
4512 Guest Rd Apt 27
Rapid City SD 57702

Call Sign: KE6YSA
Sharon D Muir
1430 Haines Ave 108 208
Rapid City SD 57701

Call Sign: KD0FTH
Frank W Rust
1430 Haines Ave 108 504
Rapid City SD 57701

Call Sign: AC0NN
Frank W Rust
1430 Haines Ave 108 504
Rapid City SD 57701

Call Sign: KB9PME
Roger L Naber
5005 Hansen Ln
Rapid City SD 577030153

Call Sign: KC0FCI
Craig A Berens
1741 Harmony Heights Ln 306
Rapid City SD 57702

Call Sign: KA0QBY
James R Kjellerson
2214 Harney Dr
Rapid City SD 57702

Call Sign: WD0EME
Clinton H Van Blaricum
2414 Harney Dr
Rapid City SD 57702

Call Sign: KD0KMV
Dan C Schaffer
616 Harter Dr
Rapid City SD 57702

Call Sign: N0ACG
John T Little
1946 Haycamp Lane
Rapid City SD 57703

Call Sign: N0OYF
Douglas E Rowe
HC 33
Rapid City SD 57701

Call Sign: WB0GDF
Richard J Stradinger
1807 Heart Ct
Rapid City SD 57701

Call Sign: N0JQK
John E Matthesen
8610 Heather Dr
Rapid City SD 57783

Call Sign: KD0AYN
Delbert R Long
1201 Herman St
Rapid City SD 57701

Call Sign: KC0FCJ
David A Cross
2416 Hidden Timbers
Rapid City SD 577021102

Call Sign: KC0ETF
Lee G Boyles
8701 Highland Hills Rd
Rapid City SD 577028954

Call Sign: K0LGB
Lee G Boyles
8701 Highland Hills Rd
Rapid City SD 577028954

Call Sign: K0STF
Jack C Brand
8703 Highland Hills Rd
Rapid City SD 57702

Call Sign: KB0ZND
Michael J Batchelder
3215 Hogan Ct
Rapid City SD 57702

Call Sign: KD0JLV
Marius D Ellingsen
4831 Homestead St Apt 205
Rapid City SD 57703

Call Sign: W0CQH
Harvey A Boyles
801 Horace Mann Dr
Rapid City SD 57701

Call Sign: KD0KRI
Niki L Wegener
808 Horace Mann Dr
Rapid City SD 57701

Call Sign: W0HYJ
Nathan J Moritz
816 Horace Mann Dr
Rapid City SD 57701

Call Sign: KC0JYU
Andy P Bormes
2405 Huntington Pl
Rapid City SD 57702

Call Sign: AB0VH
Andy P Bormes
2405 Huntington Pl
Rapid City SD 57702

Call Sign: AB0UD
Dennis W Williams
3123 Iris Dr
Rapid City SD 57702

Call Sign: N0CNH
Darwin L Behnke
2489 Jack Pine Dr
Rapid City SD 57701

Call Sign: WE1S
Craig Wilson
2218 Jackson Blvd 4821
Rapid City SD 57702

Call Sign: KC0HIB
Steve J Bauer
4106 Jackson Blvd Apt 303
Rapid City SD 577023294

Call Sign: WM1A
Carolyn M Wilson
2218 Jackson Blvd Ste 4821
Rapid City SD 577023452

Call Sign: N0NKS
Steven M Naeve
7978 Jasmine Ln
Rapid City SD 57702

Call Sign: KD0EWV
James P Devine
3143 Johnston Ct
Rapid City SD 57703

Call Sign: KC0VZW
Mitchell L Erickson
4940 Johnston Dr
Rapid City SD 57703

Call Sign: KA0ZRX
Carl R Wall
929 Joy Ave
Rapid City SD 57701

Call Sign: KC0JGE
Andy L Crawford
2317 Judy Ave
Rapid City SD 577023131

Call Sign: WA0LVE
James E Anderson
2502 Junction Dr
Rapid City SD 57701

Call Sign: KR7CQ
John A Hamilton
2518 Junction Dr
Rapid City SD 57702

Call Sign: KC0SPT
Jason D Howe
109 Kansas City St
Rapid City SD 57701

Call Sign: KA1WZY
Ian R Hardesty
124 Kansas City St
Rapid City SD 57701

Call Sign: KQ6OG
Peter K Bingham
409 Kansas City St 13
Rapid City SD 57701

Call Sign: KA0UZH
Chris Mayer
943 Kary Ln Weston Hts
Rapid City SD 57701

Call Sign: KC0PXW
Mason N Pluimer
1035 Kingswood Dr
Rapid City SD 57702

Call Sign: KC0VZP
Ryan F Kroetch
4105 Lakeview Dr 107
Rapid City SD 57702

Call Sign: KA0GRN
Dennis A Klug
3225 Leland
Rapid City SD 57701

Call Sign: KB5UMK
Michael S Marion
711 Lion Dr
Rapid City SD 57701

Call Sign: KD0IDS
Gregory M Mcdonald
2212 Lockwood Dr
Rapid City SD 57702

Call Sign: WI0C
Daniel J Mulally
6390 Long View Rd
Rapid City SD 57703

Call Sign: KB0BUT
James E Hayward Jr
7860 Long View Rd
Rapid City SD 57703

Call Sign: KB0BYT
Linda M Hayward
7860 Long View Rd
Rapid City SD 57703

Call Sign: N0KHF
Tina L Mulally
6390 Longview Rd
Rapid City SD 57703

Call Sign: KB0UYM
Amanda J Brubaker
3006 Lynnwood Ave
Rapid City SD 57701

Call Sign: KC0NDV
Roy V Best
615 Magnolia Dr
Rapid City SD 57701

Call Sign: KA9IBP
Diane M Krause
5975 Majestic Tr
Rapid City SD 57702

Call Sign: KA9GUY
Bryant D Krause
5975 Majestic Trail
Rapid City SD 57702

Call Sign: W0HYQ
Marvin A Vosika
3510 Maple
Rapid City SD 577017614

Call Sign: KB0WCG
Larry E Hudlemeyer
4615 Marcia Ct
Rapid City SD 57702

Call Sign: KB0WCH
Aaron A Hudlemeyer
4615 Marcia Ct
Rapid City SD 57702

Call Sign: K0WYC
Gerald A Snyder
3620 Margaret Ct
Rapid City SD 577020535

Call Sign: KC0MMX
Elliott B Mergler
512 Meade St
Rapid City SD 577015444

Call Sign: W6BUC
Elliott B Mergler
512 Meade St
Rapid City SD 577015444

Call Sign: WJ6Y
Elliott B Mergler
512 Meade St
Rapid City SD 577015444

Call Sign: KA0SYH
Orville D Steele
517 Meade St
Rapid City SD 57701

Call Sign: WB0BXI
David M Paulson
4109 Meadowwood
Rapid City SD 57702

Call Sign: KA0AZX
Larry V Reishus
2531 Merlot Dr
Rapid City SD 57701

Call Sign: KD0RAR
John C Boersma
352 Middle Valley Dr
Rapid City SD 57701

Call Sign: KD0KUY
Cody W Thorson
4500 Milehigh Ave
Rapid City SD 57701

Call Sign: N0BUL
Charles D Hunt
1411 Milwaukee
Rapid City SD 57701

Call Sign: N0QWZ
Ben C Sutter
2415 Minnewasta Rd
Rapid City SD 57702

Call Sign: KD5FDD
Daniel P Mc Mullen
1612 Minuteman Dr
Rapid City SD 57701

Call Sign: KA0SXI
Curt A Rosenkranz
13170 Morse Pl
Rapid City SD 577024749

Call Sign: KE6ILN
Sydney F Chavasse
1601 Mt Rushmore Rd 3 221
Rapid City SD 577014591

Call Sign: KH6TL
William S Haskell
1601 Mt Rushmore Rd 3 221
Rapid City SD 577014591

Call Sign: KD0DLA
Kenny R Umenthum
6832 Muirfield Dr
Rapid City SD 57702

Call Sign: KC0MMP
Geoffrey A Fecske
Myrtle Ave
Rapid City SD 57701

Call Sign: KA0NKL
Russell L Koch
314 N 44th
Rapid City SD 57702

Call Sign: KB0LSI
Jeffrey S Van Klompenburg
118 N 48th St
Rapid City SD 57702

Call Sign: KB0UYA
Janet L Van Klompenburg
118 N 48th St
Rapid City SD 57702

Call Sign: N0QWY
Rick A Lutz
1702 N 7th Apt 1E
Rapid City SD 57701

Call Sign: W0HJG
Lyman M Delameter
4330 N Glenview
Rapid City SD 57701

Call Sign: KC0NOF
Scott C Moses
1430 N Haines Ave Ste 108 235
Rapid City SD 577010612

Call Sign: W0YOB
Scott C Moses
1430 N Haines Ave Ste 108 235
Rapid City SD 577010612

Call Sign: N0NYA
Harold W Garwood Jr
4564 N Hwy 79 49
Rapid City SD 57702

Call Sign: KC0MVO
Gerald L Martin
4564 N Hwy79 Lot 49
Rapid City SD 57702

Call Sign: KD0FRK
Keith O Benson
716 N Spruce St
Rapid City SD 57701

Call Sign: KC0OMT
Scott L Heibel
1606 N Terrace Pl
Rapid City SD 57701

Call Sign: KB0LSB
Steven L Mangelsen
138 Nathan Ct
Rapid City SD 57701

Call Sign: KI0D
Richard G Kroes
2716 Northbrook Dr
Rapid City SD 57702

Call Sign: KA0KJE
Mark S Kjellerson
3078 O'Brien St
Rapid City SD 57703

Call Sign: N0TED
Toby K Wagner
2165 Old Farm Ct
Rapid City SD 57703

Call Sign: KC0YYL
Don E Thrall
3908 Park Dr
Rapid City SD 57702

Call Sign: KB7ZCC
Richard R Charette
4510 Patriot Lane
Rapid City SD 57701

Call Sign: KC0AFP
Kara J Knapp
222 Patton St
Rapid City SD 57701

Call Sign: KA0MXN
Richard J Hanzlik Sr
5013 Pierre St
Rapid City SD 577021836

Call Sign: N0UVO
Wayne L Boyer
1711 Plateau Ln
Rapid City SD 57701

Call Sign: WR0Q
Edward J Nelson
3134 Player Dr
Rapid City SD 577025041

Call Sign: N0IOI
Robert D Williams
5551 Pluto St
Rapid City SD 57701

Call Sign: W0HVY
Raymond A Stepanek
5622 Pluto St
Rapid City SD 57703

Call Sign: KD0IVC
Kyle J Snavely
5677 Pluto St
Rapid City SD 57703

Call Sign: WB0VIX
Jimmie M Davis
814 Polaris
Rapid City SD 57701

Call Sign: KD0JR
Todd A Warren
6906 Porthcawl Court
Rapid City SD 57702

Call Sign: N0PQE
James A Veazey
3405 Powderhorn Cir
Rapid City SD 57702

Call Sign: WA0LOG
James A Veazey
3405 Powderhorn Cir
Rapid City SD 57702

Call Sign: WB0IGV
Kevin B Goyer
4246 Range View Ct
Rapid City SD 57701

Call Sign: N0RRH
Troy E Elmstrom
1212 Rangeveiw Cir
Rapid City SD 57701

Call Sign: KC0SPS
David M Carpenter
4919 Raven Cir
Rapid City SD 57702

Call Sign: K0ALN
Vernon A Merritt
3624 Reder
Rapid City SD 57701

Call Sign: KD0NAL
Scott P Nelson
3728 Reder St
Rapid City SD 57702

Call Sign: KC0SFB
Trevor L Cash
12063 Rolling Hill Rd
Rapid City SD 57702

Call Sign: KB0YAL
David A Howard Sr
9651 Rolling Hills Dr
Rapid City SD 57702

Call Sign: WA0VDT
Willis G Howard
9663 Rolling Hills Dr
Rapid City SD 57702

Call Sign: KB0HXU
Dennis D Bahm
RR1
Rapid City SD 57702

Call Sign: K3CO
Elbert L Robberson
RR1
Rapid City SD 57702

Call Sign: KB0BYZ
Robert G Clark Jr
RR2
Rapid City SD 57701

Call Sign: KF0CQ
George D Kruse
RR8
Rapid City SD 57702

Call Sign: KB0HXV
Juanita L Clark
Rt 2
Rapid City SD 57701

Call Sign: KB0AKU
Harold R Steele
Rt 6
Rapid City SD 57701

Call Sign: W0ARC
Fred A Nicol
Rt 8
Rapid City SD 57702

Call Sign: KB0LSE
John C Knowles Jr
1603 S 7th
Rapid City SD 57701

Call Sign: N0SGR
Brian G Mitchell
113 S Berry Pine Rd
Rapid City SD 57702

Call Sign: KB0ATQ
Jay C Roman
407 S Berry Pine Rd
Rapid City SD 57702

Call Sign: KB0FTH
John C Roman
407 S Berry Pine Rd
Rapid City SD 57702

Call Sign: KA5CHI
Joseph H Muench Jr
5102 S Canyon Rd
Rapid City SD 57702

Call Sign: KC0TKM
Robert M Ragatz
5102 S Canyon Rd
Rapid City SD 57702

Call Sign: KC0SOE
Holly A Lutz
23788 S Rockerville Rd
Rapid City SD 57702

Call Sign: KC0PGP
Brian T Horton
402 S St
Rapid City SD 57701

Call Sign: KC0RYM
Joseph D Cooper
3014 S Valley Dr
Rapid City SD 57703

Call Sign: KA0SEZ
Neal H Hodges II
2327 S Valley Dr
Rapid City SD 577035997

Call Sign: K0CXL
Elmer E Meyer
715 San Marco
Rapid City SD 57701

Call Sign: KC0WQF
Nakota Communications System
705 San Marco Blvd
Rapid City SD 57702

Call Sign: KB0NRB
Robert J Streich
705 San Marco Blvd
Rapid City SD 57702

Call Sign: KB0WCF
Marjorie K Wilson
705 San Marco Blvd
Rapid City SD 57702

Call Sign: WB0PWA
Rudolph H Mooney
3030 Sandstone Ln
Rapid City SD 577015388

Call Sign: W0BLK
Black Hills Amateur Radio Club
3288 Sandstone Ln
Rapid City SD 57701

Call Sign: K0CX
Gary A Peterson
3288 Sandstone Ln
Rapid City SD 577015388

Call Sign: WB0ZCF
Loretta J Peterson
3288 Sandstone Ln
Rapid City SD 577015388

Call Sign: K0LEW
Lewis W Rohrer
408 Sapphire Lane
Rapid City SD 577016326

Call Sign: N0JFQ
Kevin E Bentch
646 Saturn Ct
Rapid City SD 57701

Call Sign: KC0EAB
Jason W Layton
9100 Schroeder Rd
Rapid City SD 577026110

Call Sign: KC0YYM
Gerald M Chaney
2802 Scott St
Rapid City SD 57703

Call Sign: K0YYM
Gerald M Chaney
2802 Scott St
Rapid City SD 57703

Call Sign: KC0TXV
Donald A Jarvinen
3641 Serendipity Ln
Rapid City SD 57702

Call Sign: K0DAJ
Donald A Jarvinen
3641 Serendipity Ln
Rapid City SD 57702

Call Sign: WA1RJC
Dale E Thomas
37 Signal Dr
Rapid City SD 57701

Call Sign: W0ZWL
Martha J Shirley
119 Signal Dr
Rapid City SD 57701

Call Sign: KD0CEU
Joseph J Birgen
719 Silver St 3
Rapid City SD 577018039

Call Sign: KC0VZQ
Stephen D Trimarchi
1107 Sitka St
Rapid City SD 577012085

Call Sign: N2FOG
Paula S Pennington
840 Spruce Lot 243
Rapid City SD 57701

Call Sign: KB0QDP
Jennifer C Burkhart
726 St Andrew
Rapid City SD 57701

Call Sign: KC5JQW
Christine M Light Ms
65 St Andrew St
Rapid City SD 57701

Call Sign: KB0SGC
Bonny S Workman
126 St Charles
Rapid City SD 57701

Call Sign: N0BJ
Bonny S Workman
126 St Charles
Rapid City SD 57701

Call Sign: N0MKD
Steven D Fletcher
613 St Charles
Rapid City SD 57701

Call Sign: KD0EWT
Eric L Klocko
237 St Cloud St
Rapid City SD 57701

Call Sign: WB0YXK
Franklin K Tomsik Sr
609 St Francis
Rapid City SD 57701

Call Sign: KC0MMV
James D Castleberry
731 St Joseph St 120
Rapid City SD 57701

Call Sign: KB0NRC
Judi L Trobee
St Patrick
Rapid City SD 57701

Call Sign: N0NVM
Catherine Griffin
2105 Stirling St
Rapid City SD 57702

Call Sign: KD0TM
Kenneth D Tomovick
23637 Strato Bowl Rd
Rapid City SD 57701

Call Sign: K0HF
Jeffrey J Halgerson
6360 Sun Ridge Rd
Rapid City SD 57702

Call Sign: KC0GWU
Catherin M Halgerson
6360 Sun Ridge Rd
Rapid City SD 57702

Call Sign: AJ4GH
Dana C Kuecker
3009 Sunny Hill Cir
Rapid City SD 57702

Call Sign: AF0DK
Dana C Kuecker
3009 Sunny Hill Cir
Rapid City SD 57702

Call Sign: KC0WNH
James L Irvine
4315 Sweetbriar St
Rapid City SD 57703

Call Sign: K0QI
James L Irvine
4315 Sweetbriar St
Rapid City SD 57703

Call Sign: KB0OUH
Gregory C Richards
826 Sycamore St
Rapid City SD 577017504

Call Sign: AC0HK
Gregory C Richards
826 Sycamore St
Rapid City SD 577017504

Call Sign: N0KT
Gregory C Richards
826 Sycamore St
Rapid City SD 577017504

Call Sign: KB0KVT
Christopher M Veazey
7283 Tanager Dr
Rapid City SD 57702

Call Sign: KB0LKT
Dennis J Olivier
14411 Tatum Ct
Rapid City SD 57701

Call Sign: KI7GL
David G Johnson
2825 Terra St
Rapid City SD 57703

Call Sign: KB0ZBP
John P Tubbs
4161 Terry Dr
Rapid City SD 57701

Call Sign: KE0IR
William C Larson
4185 Terry Dr
Rapid City SD 57701

Call Sign: WB9FWF
Edward R Pasternik
106 Texas St
Rapid City SD 57701

Call Sign: N4RLH
John B Mehaffey
13046 Timber Lane
Rapid City SD 57702

Call Sign: KA7PJQ
Betty M Smith
13064 Timber Lane
Rapid City SD 57702

Call Sign: KC7CAD
Douglas L Smith
13064 Timber Lane
Rapid City SD 57702

Call Sign: W6YQ
Michael T Hudgens Sr
5875 Timberline Rd W
Rapid City SD 57702

Call Sign: K0KLR
Gary N Johnson
6343 Timberline Rd W
Rapid City SD 57702

Call Sign: KB0BNQ
George F Freymiller
4341 Timothy St
Rapid City SD 57702

Call Sign: WD0ENO
Patrick C Gilcrease
2615 Tomahawk Dr
Rapid City SD 57702

Call Sign: W3UKO
N Addison Ball
2923 Tower Court
Rapid City SD 57701

Call Sign: KC0UXC
Charles A Conlee
4106 Troon Court
Rapid City SD 57702

Call Sign: KC0ZKD
Sarah K Conlee
4106 Troon Court
Rapid City SD 57702

Call Sign: KB0JKO
Jack W Hartinger
3825 Twilight Dr
Rapid City SD 57703

Call Sign: KC0SFC
Donald G Clayburgh
3609 Twilight Dr Lot 15
Rapid City SD 57703

Call Sign: AC0IL
Donald G Clayburgh
3609 Twilight Dr Lot 15
Rapid City SD 57703

Call Sign: WA0FUV
Robert A Ackerman
4048 Valley W Dr
Rapid City SD 577023144

Call Sign: KC0HIA
Tom A Warner
4435 W Glen Pl
Rapid City SD 57702

Call Sign: N5BGR
Robert G Allen Jr
4454 W Glen Pl
Rapid City SD 557026852

Call Sign: WB0JLX
Richard L Graves
11250 W Hwy 44
Rapid City SD 57702

Call Sign: KB0ONV
Charles R Bias
4403 W Main
Rapid City SD 57702

Call Sign: KC5EQU
Richard E Thompson
3213 W Main 403
Rapid City SD 57702

Call Sign: WB9LDT
Henry L Jones Sr
3213 W Main Box 225
Rapid City SD 57702

Call Sign: KG4NLR
Daniel W Sherwood
3213 W Main St 137
Rapid City SD 57702

Call Sign: K2KG
James A Greer
2040 W Main St 210 1668
Rapid City SD 57702

Call Sign: KD0NIM
David Katsuki
2040 W Main St 210 2198
Rapid City SD 57702

Call Sign: KJ6BXK
Carol A Escalante
2040 W Main St 210 2805
Rapid City SD 57702

Call Sign: KJ6BXJ
Steven J Escalante
2040 W Main St 210 2805
Rapid City SD 577022570

Call Sign: KC0OJL
Daniel E Wainwright
3213 W Main St 248
Rapid City SD 577022314

Call Sign: KC0RVO
Vicki M Thompson
3213 W Main St 403
Rapid City SD 57702

Call Sign: K9ESO
Scott U Adam
3213 W Main St 614
Rapid City SD 577022314

Call Sign: KF6RVB
Jean S Adam
3213 W Main St 614
Rapid City SD 577022314

Call Sign: KC0MXE
John W Fenn
3213 W Main St Pmb 204
Rapid City SD 577022314

Call Sign: KD0GCA
John E Burgan
2040 W Main St Ste 210 2065
Rapid City SD 57702

Call Sign: KC0UNN
David L Kolbo Jr
2040 W Main St Ste 210 2240
Rapid City SD 577022570

Call Sign: KD0IDE
Kristina R Lippke
2040 W Main St Ste 210 2248
Rapid City SD 57702

Call Sign: AC0PI
David L Lippke
2040 W Main St Ste 210 2248
Rapid City SD 57702

Call Sign: KD0IJD
Randall W Moe
2040 W Main St Ste 210 2375
Rapid City SD 57702

Call Sign: KD0LTU
Gordon S Gore
2040 W Main St Ste 210 2736
Rapid City SD 577022570

Call Sign: KC0JOR
Jeffrey H Wiswall
2525 W Main St Ste 307
Rapid City SD 57702

Call Sign: WB0BRO
Ernest F Meiers
3911 W Omaha
Rapid City SD 57702

Call Sign: KA0ZYP
Theodore H Kozlik
3631 W Omaha St
Rapid City SD 577022378

Call Sign: KA0FTA
Robert A Morgan
2817 W St Anne
Rapid City SD 57702

Call Sign: KC0PGQ
Aaron L Goehring
624 Waterloo
Rapid City SD 57701

Call Sign: N0PSW
Ronald J Olsen Jr
871 Waterloo Apt 2
Rapid City SD 57701

Call Sign: WB0NGP
Daniel L Kennison
608 Wayside Dr
Rapid City SD 57702

Call Sign: K0DLK
Daniel L Kennison
608 Wayside Dr
Rapid City SD 57702

Call Sign: WB0FXO
Richard C Geib
609 Wayside Dr
Rapid City SD 57701

Call Sign: KD0KMU
Kent E Renaud
203 Wedgewood Dr
Rapid City SD 57702

Call Sign: KD0NYK
Mark D Armstrong
6548 Wellington Dr
Rapid City SD 57702

Call Sign: KC0VZR
Jeffrey J Schild
6633 Wellington Dr
Rapid City SD 57702

Call Sign: KD0FRJ
Edwin Noble
4530 Wentworth Dr
Rapid City SD 57702

Call Sign: K0OLW
Edwin Noble
4530 Wentworth Dr
Rapid City SD 57702

Call Sign: KD0FRI
Shirley J Noble
4530 Wentworth Dr
Rapid City SD 57702

Call Sign: K0SJN
Shirley J Noble
4530 Wentworth Dr
Rapid City SD 57702

Call Sign: KB7PLI
Dwight R Pladsen
4571 Wentworth Dr
Rapid City SD 577021990

Call Sign: KE7KK
William B Kipping
524 Westberry Dr
Rapid City SD 57702

Call Sign: WD0B
David C Bartsch
23626 Wilderness Canyon Rd
Rapid City SD 57702

Call Sign: KC0LOB
Keith W Whites
23633 Wilderness Canyon Rd
Rapid City SD 57702

Call Sign: N8NKP
Duane L Abata
23632 Wilderness Canyon Rd
Rapid City SD 57702

Call Sign: KB0LSD
Michael J Bowers
5575 Wildwood Dr
Rapid City SD 57702

Call Sign: KB0PBO
Timothy A Hutchinson
2821 Wilkie Dr Apt 103
Rapid City SD 57702

Call Sign: KB2VSL
Lilly Jones
2815 Willow Ave
Rapid City SD 57701

Call Sign: N0SGS
Dennis R Wilkins
2316 Wisconsin Ave
Rapid City SD 57701

Call Sign: N0XYH
Linda M Wilkins
2316 Wisconsin Ave
Rapid City SD 57701

Call Sign: KC0MMW
Jason J Nemeth
3113 Wisconsin Ave
Rapid City SD 57701

Call Sign: KD0DLD
David A Roth
4102 Wonderland Dr
Rapid City SD 57702

Call Sign: N0QXA
Edward R Trigg
Wood
Rapid City SD 57701

Call Sign: WB0GID
Marvin G Telkamp
13084 Woodland Ct
Rapid City SD 57702

Call Sign: N7HFO
Vance S Schauer
1064 Ziebach St
Rapid City SD 577030174

Call Sign: WB0FUV
Henry J Cretsinger
Rapid City SD 57709

Call Sign: KD0DGS
Pennington Co Search And Rescue
Radio Club
Rapid City SD 57709

Call Sign: KD0LUX
Rmtkkt Arc
Rapid City SD 57709

Call Sign: K0ZUN
John L Shaffer
Rapid City SD 57709

Call Sign: K4FBE
Thomas R Monheim
Rapid City SD 57709

Call Sign: KB0PLZ
Joseph R Tippmann
Rapid City SD 57709

Call Sign: W5SWI
Archie L Lee
Rapid City SD 57709

Call Sign: KD0FRH
Jazek C Kraemer
Rapid City SD 57709

Call Sign: N0EDI
Peter B Linde
Rapid City SD 577090711

Call Sign: N0XYF
Norman W Pierce

Rapid City SD 577092461

Call Sign: N0TAA
Sara E Schelske
309 E 16th Ave
Redfield SD 57469

Call Sign: WD0BIA
Gary R Schelske
309 E 16th Ave
Redfield SD 57469

Call Sign: KB0HHI
Herbert H Jockheck
1115 E 1st St
Redfield SD 57469

Call Sign: K0ASQ
Eugene Versteeg
1202 E 1st St
Redfield SD 57469

Call Sign: N0SDF
Robert F Cartner
1404 E 1st St
Redfield SD 57469

Call Sign: WG0F
Michael B Lesselyoung
302 E 1st St
Redfield SD 574691214

Call Sign: KA0IXX
Connie L Morrison
708 E 7th Ave
Redfield SD 57469

Call Sign: WD0BIB
Susan I Schelske
RR2
Redfield SD 57469

Call Sign: KA0UEJ
Donald A L Harriott
Rt 2
Redfield SD 57469

Call Sign: KB0UEL
Kevin K Roseland
17278 US Hwy 281
Redfield SD 57469

Call Sign: W0IER
David J Keller
911 W 5th St
Redfield SD 57469

Call Sign: KB0CGW
Timothy D Marlette
110 W 7th Ave
Redfield SD 57469

Call Sign: KB0BHQ
Doyal E Wall
Redfield SD 57469

Call Sign: WA0ZWZ
Gary E Moore
Redfield SD 57469

Call Sign: KC0QYH
Michelle M Stadel
Redfield SD 57469

FCC Amateur Radio Licenses in Reliance

Call Sign: WB0HTT
Carrol I Stewart
32830 246th St
Reliance SD 57569

Call Sign: N0SUT
Scott L Wagner
32981 248th St
Reliance SD 57569

Call Sign: N0YZL
Colton W Thelen
HCR 4
Reliance SD 57569

FCC Amateur Radio Licenses in Renner

Call Sign: KA0DOA
David L Bacon
47479 258th St
Renner SD 57055

Call Sign: KC0FZM
Dennis L Hoffman
25755 475th Ave
Renner SD 570556504

Call Sign: KC0EVT
Don L Mitchell
25752 Lindbergh Ave
Renner SD 57055

FCC Amateur Radio Licenses in Reva

Call Sign: KD0KMT
Brandon E Tenold
Reva SD 57651

Call Sign: KD0KMS
Dustin R Tenold
Reva SD 57651

FCC Amateur Radio Licenses in Revillo

Call Sign: N0XPF
Jo Ann P Hunt
RR1
Revillo SD 57259

Call Sign: KB0LSH
Allis Alexander
Revillo SD 57259

FCC Amateur Radio Licenses in Ridgeview

Call Sign: K0GSY
Theodore E Rousseau
Ridgeview SD 57652

FCC Amateur Radio Licenses in Roscoe

Call Sign: WB0LWE
Candis J Kub
35036 141st Sreet
Roscoe SD 57471

Call Sign: K0GZ
Raymond J Kub
35036 141st St
Roscoe SD 574717003

FCC Amateur Radio Licenses in Rosholt

Call Sign: N0YSI
Daniel R Hunter
Rosholt SD 57260

FCC Amateur Radio Licenses in Rutland

Call Sign: KB0HHA
Irvin M Johnson
Rutland SD 57057

FCC Amateur Radio Licenses in Saint Francis

Call Sign: WB3HPU
Richard H Harris
Saint Francis SD 57572

FCC Amateur Radio Licenses in Salem

Call Sign: KC0DZI
Raymond P Spildener
43668 252nd St
Salem SD 57058

Call Sign: WA0UFS
Edith M Gray
43804 257 St
Salem SD 570585907

Call Sign: W0OE
Edith M Gray
43804 257 St
Salem SD 570585907

Call Sign: KD0DXB
Carmine Meoli
43804 257th St
Salem SD 57058

Call Sign: W0SD
Edward C Gray
43804 257th St
Salem SD 570585907

Call Sign: W6PPB
John W Boggess
221 S Main
Salem SD 57058

FCC Amateur Radio Licenses in Scotland

Call Sign: KB0TLB
Gayle D Dunn
Scotland SD 57059

Call Sign: KC0VWU
Richard Struck
Scotland SD 57059

Call Sign: NZ2N
Richard Struck
Scotland SD 57059

FCC Amateur Radio Licenses in Selby

Call Sign: WB0YDG
Milton F Schauer
SR
Selby SD 57472

Call Sign: W0ADZ
Christian L Stallkamp
210 W Scranton
Selby SD 57472

Call Sign: KA0LOI
Donald L Steder
Selby SD 57472

Call Sign: WB0ZZH
Charles W Davidson
Selby SD 57472

FCC Amateur Radio Licenses in Shadehill

Call Sign: KB0GFK
Caleb J Wiechmann
HCR 67
Shadehill SD 57653

FCC Amateur Radio Licenses in Silver City

Call Sign: N0QWI
Jeffrey C Sugrue
205 Duggan St
Silver City SD 577026028

FCC Amateur Radio Licenses in Sinai

Call Sign: KA0DEJ
Marcus S Eastby
Sinai SD 57061

FCC Amateur Radio Licenses in Sioux Falls

Call Sign: WB0WNS
Terry D Steenholdt
46818 263rd St
Sioux Falls SD 571077012

Call Sign: K0SZJ
Walter L Bruns
3405 E 11th St 12
Sioux Falls SD 57103

Call Sign: KC0DNH
Daniel J Koskela
25841 471st Ave
Sioux Falls SD 57107

Call Sign: KB0WUG
Anthony G Johnson
1400 E 12th St
Sioux Falls SD 57103

Call Sign: K0QOW
Alfred E Hartmann
1808 Arrowhead Pass
Sioux Falls SD 57103

Call Sign: KC0RFR
John P Hanson
1402 E 12th St
Sioux Falls SD 57103

Call Sign: KA0ARO
Ward B Whitwam
1204 Cedar Pl
Sioux Falls SD 57103

Call Sign: KB0TTC
Duane J Lorenz
405 E 12th St 109
Sioux Falls SD 57104

Call Sign: N0ACL
Bryce R Whitwam
1204 Cedar Pl
Sioux Falls SD 57103

Call Sign: KD0QYQ
Becky M Odegaard
405 E 12th St 109
Sioux Falls SD 57104

Call Sign: WB0OQZ
Wayne B Whitwam
1204 Cedar Pl
Sioux Falls SD 57105

Call Sign: W0GDE
Ralph E Macy
614 E 13th St Apt 105
Sioux Falls SD 57104

Call Sign: N0ABE
Roland L Johnson
1321 Coates Rd
Sioux Falls SD 57105

Call Sign: N0OXU
James A Moeller
1412 E 16
Sioux Falls SD 57104

Call Sign: KD0ICI
Michael J Kent
5108 Daffodil Cir
Sioux Falls SD 57108

Call Sign: KD0IIV
Charles S Henson
3009 E 17th St
Sioux Falls SD 57103

Call Sign: NF0H
Michael J Kent
5108 Daffodil Cir
Sioux Falls SD 57108

Call Sign: KB0ECO
Chan B Masselink
104 E 20th
Sioux Falls SD 57105

Call Sign: W0ZIQ
Donald T Meisel
101 E 27th St
Sioux Falls SD 57105

Call Sign: KC0VHB
Michael J Oimoen
601 E 28th St
Sioux Falls SD 57105

Call Sign: KA0QHY
Beverly A Mondt
4419 E 28th St
Sioux Falls SD 57103

Call Sign: WB0ORW
Miles S Mondt
4419 E 28th St
Sioux Falls SD 57103

Call Sign: WA0RPT
Robert L Shuck
3401 E 31st
Sioux Falls SD 57103

Call Sign: KC0RXC
Paul N Wilson
4605 E 33rd
Sioux Falls SD 57110

Call Sign: WB0ILT
Philip H Ream
1412 E 33rd St
Sioux Falls SD 571055105

Call Sign: KA0KPY
Warner H Muns
204 E 35th St
Sioux Falls SD 571054937

Call Sign: WB0OQP
Harry M Benjamin Jr
604 E 35th St
Sioux Falls SD 57105

Call Sign: N0SFB
Wendell R De Geus
1818 E 3rd St Apt 312
Sioux Falls SD 571031041

Call Sign: KI0BV
Terry D Texley
4912 E 42nd St
Sioux Falls SD 57110

Call Sign: KB0YRI
David C Harms
711 E 4th St
Sioux Falls SD 57103

Call Sign: N0SHY
Melody E Jewell
2100 E 58th St
Sioux Falls SD 57108

Call Sign: K9BU
James G Jenson
1204 E 67th St N
Sioux Falls SD 57104

Call Sign: KB0SJH
Thomas K Mc Donald
1806 E 7th St
Sioux Falls SD 57103

Call Sign: KD0EHS
Clarence C Williams
3909 E 7th St
Sioux Falls SD 57103

Call Sign: KD0DLW
Randall G Williams
3909 E 7th St
Sioux Falls SD 57103

Call Sign: W8LMC
Lawrence M Cain
1401 E 7th St Apt 7
Sioux Falls SD 57103

Call Sign: N3TQX
James P Throne
401 E 8th St Ste 214 240
Sioux Falls SD 57103

Call Sign: KC0ZDB
Richard C Scheit
401 E 8th St Ste 214 333
Sioux Falls SD 571037008

Call Sign: N0ALW
Tanner J Daniel
401 E 8th St Ste 214 373
Sioux Falls SD 57103

Call Sign: W0TJD
Tanner J Daniel
401 E 8th St Ste 214 373
Sioux Falls SD 57103

Call Sign: N0RPZ
Lawrence W Hecht
1012 E 9th St
Sioux Falls SD 57103

Call Sign: KC0PMB
Donald E Morin
4812 E Belmont St
Sioux Falls SD 571106933

Call Sign: KB0HDP
Matthew D Frederes
2108 E Briar Den Ct
Sioux Falls SD 571085118

Call Sign: KD0QYR
Dustin J Schnabel
5120 E Fernwood Dr
Sioux Falls SD 57110

Call Sign: KD0IPE
Andrew J Austin
5216 E Fernwood Dr
Sioux Falls SD 57110

Call Sign: KA2MHY
Mark K Huntington Sr
8600 E Hidden Valley Rd
Sioux Falls SD 57110

Call Sign: KD0KTZ
Jay J Trobec
1008 E Jenny Cir
Sioux Falls SD 57108

Call Sign: KE0JAY
Jay J Trobec
1008 E Jenny Cir
Sioux Falls SD 57108

Call Sign: KB0RIA
Michael A Forinash
224 E Pam Rd
Sioux Falls SD 571055840

Call Sign: KB0UPT
Christopher C Anderson
1613 E Ponderosa Dr
Sioux Falls SD 57103

Call Sign: WA0OUR
Norman C Anderson
1613 E Ponderosa Dr
Sioux Falls SD 57103

Call Sign: KD0OKO
David E Satterness
6016 E Powder House Cir
Sioux Falls SD 57110

Call Sign: AC0KW
Corwyn R Meyer
3820 E Ronning Dr
Sioux Falls SD 57103

Call Sign: KC0DAT
Connie A Gustafson
4401 E Scranton St
Sioux Falls SD 571036643

Call Sign: WB0HHM
Raymond P Gustafson
4401 E Scranton St
Sioux Falls SD 571036643

Call Sign: N0IKS
Christopher M Kappenman
606 Eagle Pl
Sioux Falls SD 57107

Call Sign: KC0UWD
Thomas D Ebaugh
1908 Fox Trail
Sioux Falls SD 57103

Call Sign: N0PSZ
Jason S Job
1013 Gordon Dr
Sioux Falls SD 57103

Call Sign: KA0NKP
Judith K Menage
1501 Gordon Dr
Sioux Falls SD 571103752

Call Sign: KB0SJI
Jeff A Wingert
1245 Holly Ave
Sioux Falls SD 57104

Call Sign: KC0TJN
James P Kilian
1905 Hunters Cir
Sioux Falls SD 57103

Call Sign: KC0NQI
Joseph A Lamoreux
810 Irene Pl
Sioux Falls SD 57107

Call Sign: KC0USQ
James Dietz
3504 Jesse James Dr
Sioux Falls SD 57103

Call Sign: KC0JKY
Cynthia L Wilson
400 Jolyn Dr
Sioux Falls SD 571083802

Call Sign: N0XBH
David L Danielson
2482 Kenwood Manor 4
Sioux Falls SD 571044472

Call Sign: KA0UEM
Arthur H Johnshoy
3904 Kris Dr
Sioux Falls SD 57103

Call Sign: KA0OFA
Ross Ortman
11301 Kuhle Dr
Sioux Falls SD 57107

Call Sign: N0VYT
Keith L Porter
3608 Marion Rd
Sioux Falls SD 57106

Call Sign: N7ZKL
Thomas G Griffin III
2515441 Metavante Way
Sioux Falls SD 57186

Call Sign: KD0TE
Steven D Ahrendt
2609 Minnehaha Dr
Sioux Falls SD 571053325

Call Sign: W4AQI
Paul N Wilson
1001 N Barnard Ave
Sioux Falls SD 57110

Call Sign: N7SCR
Daniel R Ray
925 N Blauvelt
Sioux Falls SD 57103

Call Sign: WA0SBR
Edward O Eastwold
42 N Cactus Pl
Sioux Falls SD 571106429

Call Sign: WA0NQO
Gary E Holman
1105 N Connor Trail
Sioux Falls SD 57103

Call Sign: KC0VDF
Donald R Saxton Jr
200 N Detroit Ave
Sioux Falls SD 57110

Call Sign: K0RIK
Ricky A Rackow
420 N Duluth Ave
Sioux Falls SD 57104

Call Sign: AB0ZR
Sheldon L Hendricks
1113 N Elmwood Ave
Sioux Falls SD 57104

Call Sign: N0JPV
Richard L Beebe III
426 N Fairfax Ave
Sioux Falls SD 571030822

Call Sign: WD0ETU
Richard H Stammer Sr
520 N Franklin Ave
Sioux Falls SD 571030828

Call Sign: KC0PMA
James E Lynch
515 N Grange Ave
Sioux Falls SD 57104

Call Sign: WB0ZYC
James E Lynch
515 N Grange Ave
Sioux Falls SD 57104

Call Sign: KG0MW
Chad E Phillips
504 N Grange Ave
Sioux Falls SD 57104

Call Sign: KD0ICJ
Thomas J Langpap
1425 N Holbrook Ave
Sioux Falls SD 57107

Call Sign: N0TJL
Thomas J Langpap
1425 N Holbrook Ave
Sioux Falls SD 57107

Call Sign: KB0GDH
Neal L Goldammer
101 N Holly Apt 111
Sioux Falls SD 57104

Call Sign: WA0IDW
Ronald E Glawe Sr
5501 N La Mesa Dr
Sioux Falls SD 57107

Call Sign: KC0IYC
Warren E Glawe
5501 N Lamesa Dr
Sioux Falls SD 57107

Call Sign: KD0KTY
Robert P Dykstra
616 N Leadale Ave
Sioux Falls SD 57103

Call Sign: KB0GIQ
Ronald E Johnson
414 N Linwood Crt
Sioux Falls SD 571031129

Call Sign: KC0TQW
Matthew P Kappel
710 N Montgomery Ct
Sioux Falls SD 57103

Call Sign: KC0JOK
Daniel J Ruesch
300 N Sandberg Dr
Sioux Falls SD 57103

Call Sign: KB0A
Clay H Forrette
3101 N Six Mile Rd
Sioux Falls SD 571107303

Call Sign: N0DFJ
Norma J Forrette
3101 N Six Mile Rd
Sioux Falls SD 571107303

Call Sign: N0HIS
Darrin L Tille
3103 N Six Mile Rd
Sioux Falls SD 57110

Call Sign: KA0PQX
Jean L Miller
1100 N Summit Ave
Sioux Falls SD 571041429

Call Sign: N5MYF
John C Kelly
620 N Sycamore Ave Apt 102
Sioux Falls SD 571105804

Call Sign: KA0IAP
Robert C Mc Gilvray
301 N Wayland Ave
Sioux Falls SD 571031423

Call Sign: K0BSY
Duane R Kuntz
805 N Williams Ave
Sioux Falls SD 571041931

Call Sign: KC0MBA
Thomas G Jones II
4409 Northridge Cir
Sioux Falls SD 57105

Call Sign: AB0TV
Thomas G Jones II
4409 Northridge Cir
Sioux Falls SD 57105

Call Sign: KC0OCN
Chad K Jones
4409 Northridge Cir
Sioux Falls SD 57105

Call Sign: K0JVD
William L Estlund
6205 Oscar Howe Cir
Sioux Falls SD 57106

Call Sign: KN0M
Steve C Sugrue
3008 Patrick Pl
Sioux Falls SD 57105

Call Sign: N8DXV
Donald F Gilbert
3408 Ralph Rogers Rd Apt 207C
Sioux Falls SD 57106

Call Sign: WD8NYL
Lois I Gilbert
3408 Ralph Rogers Rd Apt 207C
Sioux Falls SD 571062626

Call Sign: N0SGW
Eric D Daggett
512 Rohl Dr
Sioux Falls SD 57103

Call Sign: N0AZV
J Keith Connelly
808 Rohl Dr
Sioux Falls SD 57103

Call Sign: KB0AUA
Dennis W Robinson
RR3
Sioux Falls SD 57106

Call Sign: N0IHG
Richard V Johnson
1203 S 2nd Ave
Sioux Falls SD 57105

Call Sign: KA0SDB
Rick O Johnson
2800 S 2nd Ave
Sioux Falls SD 57105

Call Sign: WA0ECK
Harry A De Velde
2901 S 2nd Ave
Sioux Falls SD 57105

Call Sign: KB0GEO
Charles P Reagan
1205 S 4th Ave
Sioux Falls SD 57105

Call Sign: KA0CMG
Chris R Forman
3212 S 5th Ave
Sioux Falls SD 57105

Call Sign: N0BOM
Richard W Forman
3212 S 5th Ave
Sioux Falls SD 57105

Call Sign: N0JOY
Paul W Kock
601 S 69th St Apt 124
Sioux Falls SD 57108

Call Sign: N0DNS
David E Cole
1730 S 7th Ave
Sioux Falls SD 571052035

Call Sign: KC0UYT
Iver W Mercer
6000 S Aaron Ave
Sioux Falls SD 57106

Call Sign: W0EDK
Edward A Kraayenhof
6120 S Aaron Ave
Sioux Falls SD 571062673

Call Sign: KD0MVL
Eric R Ortega
1720 S Aberdeen Cir
Sioux Falls SD 57106

Call Sign: N3TUX
Eric R Ortega
1720 S Aberdeen Cir
Sioux Falls SD 57106

Call Sign: N0VBW
Todd A Heitkamp
3512 S Anita Ave
Sioux Falls SD 57103

Call Sign: N0LNQ
Jack A Carlson
1325 S Annway Dr
Sioux Falls SD 571033538

Call Sign: KC0DJU
Jody C Rundell
4309 S Arden Cir
Sioux Falls SD 57103

Call Sign: KC0RXB
Tofan M Ashraf
2505 S Aseot Ave
Sioux Falls SD 57103

Call Sign: KE0AL
Douglas B Grinsell
2308 S Avondale Ave
Sioux Falls SD 571105608

Call Sign: KB0MWQ
Gerard M Horger
4800 S Baneberry Dr
Sioux Falls SD 57106

Call Sign: WB0YQT
Toby J Wellenstein
2301 S Beacon Pl
Sioux Falls SD 571033379

Call Sign: KD0DLZ
Robert M Jenkins
2705 S Bernhaven Ave
Sioux Falls SD 57110

Call Sign: WD0CWI
Donald B Seiler
3201 S Bingen Ave
Sioux Falls SD 57110

Call Sign: KC0NZL
David B Fancher
4500 S Birchwood Ave
Sioux Falls SD 57103

Call Sign: KA0TVT
Brian J Overgard
517 S Blaine Ave
Sioux Falls SD 57103

Call Sign: N0CWG
Kelly J Anderson
619 S Blaine Ave
Sioux Falls SD 57103

Call Sign: N0KQF
David L Stangeland
2505 S Blauvelt Ave
Sioux Falls SD 57105

Call Sign: N0TIU
Lori A Stangeland
2505 S Blauvelt Ave
Sioux Falls SD 57105

Call Sign: KA0QNS
James W Kurvink
2601 S Blauvelt Ave
Sioux Falls SD 57105

Call Sign: KA0VME
Edward A Kraayenhof
2008 S Bradford Ct
Sioux Falls SD 571065340

Call Sign: N0KGZ
Steven C Wehling
3608 S Cathy 2
Sioux Falls SD 57106

Call Sign: N0HJI
Wesley J Tschetter Jr
1509 S Center
Sioux Falls SD 57103

Call Sign: KB0MYN
Gary E Graves
1601 S Center Ave
Sioux Falls SD 57105

Call Sign: KD0LRV
Michael G Best
5500 S Chuck Dr
Sioux Falls SD 57108

Call Sign: AA0GI
Dale E Misterek
5600 S Chuck Dr
Sioux Falls SD 57108

Call Sign: WD0CTM
Nancy K Neve
922 S Cleveland
Sioux Falls SD 57103

Call Sign: KD0QMK
Jerry R Warmbein
904 S Cleveland Ave
Sioux Falls SD 57103

Call Sign: WD0EDV
Gerald J Neve
922 S Cleveland Ave
Sioux Falls SD 57103

Call Sign: KB0PHA
Robb A Meert
1721 S Cliff
Sioux Falls SD 57105

Call Sign: WB0YFG
James H Meert Jr
1721 S Cliff
Sioux Falls SD 57105

Call Sign: KB0TFO
Matthew J Meert
1721 S Cliff Ave
Sioux Falls SD 57105

Call Sign: W0TRI
Tri Star Amateur Radio Club
304 S Conklin Ave 9
Sioux Falls SD 57103

Call Sign: KC0JMN
Tri Star Amateur Radio Club
304 S Conklin Ave 9
Sioux Falls SD 571031952

Call Sign: KC0EAO
Daniel S Starkenburg
304 S Conklin Ave Apt 12
Sioux Falls SD 57103

Call Sign: KB0YSW
Brian A Roth
7213 S Connie Ave
Sioux Falls SD 57108

Call Sign: KC0MVF
Jason A Meyer
7405 S Connie Ave
Sioux Falls SD 57108

Call Sign: WD0ASE
Marlin R Vetter
2309 S Crown Hill Dr
Sioux Falls SD 57106

Call Sign: KE9CS
Kenneth W Dicks
515 S Dakota Ave Ste 11 201
Sioux Falls SD 57104

Call Sign: AC0GV
Kenneth W Dicks
515 S Dakota Ave Ste 11 201
Sioux Falls SD 57104

Call Sign: KE0KN
Arnold J Spadino
601 S Duluth Ave
Sioux Falls SD 57104

Call Sign: KC0OVW
Todd R Curtis
3507 S Duluth Ave
Sioux Falls SD 57105

Call Sign: K9KFC
Todd R Curtis
3507 S Duluth Ave
Sioux Falls SD 57105

Call Sign: KB0QCV
Lester W Wilson
1125 S Ebenezer Ave Apt 318
Sioux Falls SD 57106

Call Sign: W0LLW
Lester W Wilson
1125 S Ebenezer Ave Apt 318
Sioux Falls SD 57106

Call Sign: W0LWW
Lester W Wilson
1125 S Ebenezer Ave Apt 318
Sioux Falls SD 57106

Call Sign: WB0NPT
Warren J Mc Lain
1000 S Fawn Ct
Sioux Falls SD 57110

Call Sign: KD0NZK
Troy C Clavel
5812 S Frontier Trail
Sioux Falls SD 57108

Call Sign: KD0ZP
Glen R Wittrock
3544 S Gateway Blvd Apt 202
Sioux Falls SD 57106

Call Sign: K0TQM
William B Congdon
2816 S Glendale
Sioux Falls SD 57105

Call Sign: N0LPO
Rosemarie Beebe
913 S Gordon Dr
Sioux Falls SD 57110

Call Sign: KC0JZL
Alyssa E Damiata
913 S Gordon Dr
Sioux Falls SD 57110

Call Sign: KC0MKF
Dana N Beebe
913 S Gordon Dr
Sioux Falls SD 57110

Call Sign: N0PV
Rosemarie Beebe
913 S Gordon Dr
Sioux Falls SD 57110

Call Sign: N0BOU
Richard W Menage
1501 S Gordon Dr
Sioux Falls SD 571103752

Call Sign: N0PV
Richard L Beebe III
913 S Gordon Dr
Sioux Falls SD 571103151

Call Sign: WD0CVY
Lance C Nygaard
3500 S Grace Cir
Sioux Falls SD 571037226

Call Sign: W0GFS
Jaron C Zastrow
115 S Grange Ave
Sioux Falls SD 57104

Call Sign: WB0WJH
Steven R Zastrow
115 S Grange Ave
Sioux Falls SD 57104

Call Sign: WV0K
Philip M Borgum
2510 S Grange Ave
Sioux Falls SD 57105

Call Sign: WY0Z
Larry E Hofmeister
8124 S Grass Creek Dr
Sioux Falls SD 57108

Call Sign: KA5GEI
Mark G Yarbrough
2713 S Groveland Ave
Sioux Falls SD 57110

Call Sign: K0LXE
Darrold W Morey
3212 S Hawthorne
Sioux Falls SD 57105

Call Sign: K0ROG
Roger L Kehm
2610 S Hawthorne Ave
Sioux Falls SD 571054512

Call Sign: KX6S
Eugene R Seiler
4405 S Hickory Hill Rd
Sioux Falls SD 57103

Call Sign: KC0MKE
Patricia A Ruha
812 S Highland Ave
Sioux Falls SD 571032211

Call Sign: KB0U
James H Meert
2604 S Holly Ave
Sioux Falls SD 57105

Call Sign: KD0QMO
Audrey R Mcreavy
604 S Horizon Ln
Sioux Falls SD 57106

Call Sign: KD0QML
Jerry A Mcreavy
604 S Horizon Ln
Sioux Falls SD 57106

Call Sign: WA3RVJ
Sanford L Silverberg
4901 S Jasmine Trail
Sioux Falls SD 571082826

Call Sign: KB0MND
Doris F Conradson
3408 S Judy Ave
Sioux Falls SD 571037255

Call Sign: KE0YX
Glen D Conradson
3408 S Judy Ave
Sioux Falls SD 571037255

Call Sign: K0SXB
Glen D Conradson
3408 S Judy Ave
Sioux Falls SD 571037255

Call Sign: KD5HMM
Sheri L Zimmel
1700 S Larkspur Trl
Sioux Falls SD 57106

Call Sign: KC0YMW
Daniel C Simon
5308 S Lewis
Sioux Falls SD 57108

Call Sign: K0ZOE
Daniel C Simon
5308 S Lewis
Sioux Falls SD 57108

Call Sign: WD9GMG
Douglas E Benedict
4304 S Lewis Ave
Sioux Falls SD 57103

Call Sign: KC4ASW
Karl J Harris
1000 S Liberty Pl
Sioux Falls SD 57106

Call Sign: N0YRT
Shane A Morey
4304 S Lisanne Ave
Sioux Falls SD 571037638

Call Sign: N0RCY
Walter R Marty
2507 S Lockwood Pl
Sioux Falls SD 57105

Call Sign: W0SMV
Dale E Russell
7400 S Louise Ave
Sioux Falls SD 571085913

Call Sign: KD0QMP
Chad R Nielsen
4004 S Louise Ave 306
Sioux Falls SD 57106

Call Sign: KB0WUF
Garret M Davis
300 S Lowell 15
Sioux Falls SD 57103

Call Sign: KC0MBB
Vincent A Nesheim
404 S Lowell Ave
Sioux Falls SD 57103

Call Sign: N0OXT
Richard W Draeger
1200 S Lyndale Ave
Sioux Falls SD 57105

Call Sign: W0LXQ
Ross S Fenn
1315 S Main Ave
Sioux Falls SD 57105

Call Sign: WD0EXR
Jeffrey M Ball
2014 S Main Ave
Sioux Falls SD 57105

Call Sign: N0APA
Robert H Rich
3700 S Marion Rd
Sioux Falls SD 57106

Call Sign: W0LX
Alfred M Gowan
3901 S Marion Rd
Sioux Falls SD 57106

Call Sign: N1ORZ
Stephen R Carson
1404 S Marion Rd 106
Sioux Falls SD 57106

Call Sign: KC0RXD
Michael R Hagert
1913 S Melanie Ln
Sioux Falls SD 57103

Call Sign: K0EWG
Michael R Hagert
1913 S Melanie Ln
Sioux Falls SD 57103

Call Sign: WB0RHJ
Jay A Heath
2008 S Melanie Ln
Sioux Falls SD 57103

Call Sign: KE0Z
Willis L Gravning
119 S Menlo Ave
Sioux Falls SD 57104

Call Sign: KD0PIN
Justin J Hager
7304 S Moor Cross Dr
Sioux Falls SD 57108

Call Sign: KC0RWU
John A Daniels
4609 S Nathan Ave
Sioux Falls SD 57103

Call Sign: KD0JYD
Cynda K Jones
4409 S Northridge Cir
Sioux Falls SD 57105

Call Sign: N0XQF
Erna M Jantzen
4900 S Oxbow Ave Apt 210
Sioux Falls SD 57106

Call Sign: KA0ETV
Thomas V Schulte
2212 S Oxford Ave
Sioux Falls SD 57106

Call Sign: KA0ETW
Carol D Schulte
2212 S Oxford Ave
Sioux Falls SD 57106

Call Sign: K9VKG
David L Haigh
410 S Phillips Ave
Sioux Falls SD 57104

Call Sign: N0LRU
Tom M Gage
2009 S Phillips Ave
Sioux Falls SD 57105

Call Sign: WD0GXP
Dwaine M Bogenhagen
400 S Prairie Apt 10
Sioux Falls SD 57104

Call Sign: N0KHP
Jill E Whitley
1613 S Purdue Ave
Sioux Falls SD 57106

Call Sign: KC0QVZ
Erick J Howe
708 S Regal Pl
Sioux Falls SD 57106

Call Sign: KC0TLU
Brian L Klavetter
505 S Rohl Dr
Sioux Falls SD 57103

Call Sign: KC0PLZ
John C Phillips
406 S Saint Paul Ave
Sioux Falls SD 57103

Call Sign: KB0MRF
Robert W Hinkhouse
5413 S Sarmar Ave
Sioux Falls SD 57106

Call Sign: WF0BBM
William J Feezell
5604 S Sarmar Ave
Sioux Falls SD 57106

Call Sign: KC0YVS
William J Feezell
5604 S Sarmar Ave
Sioux Falls SD 57106

Call Sign: N0MAU
Jeffrey C Kline
2710 S Sertoma Ave
Sioux Falls SD 57106

Call Sign: WA0OYT
Rex Grimme
3430 S Sheldon Ave 201
Sioux Falls SD 57105

Call Sign: KB5ZAU
Chesley H Cain
1312 S Snyder Cir
Sioux Falls SD 57106

Call Sign: K0CLT
Donald J Barnett
3600 S Spencer Blvd
Sioux Falls SD 57103

Call Sign: WA0PBL
Fred W Lehmann
1521 S Spring
Sioux Falls SD 57105

Call Sign: N0KAE
Judith E Stoakes
1010 S Stoakes Ave
Sioux Falls SD 57103

Call Sign: N0IHX
Gary K Stoakes
1010 S Stoakes Ave
Sioux Falls SD 57110

Call Sign: WA0TCW
Joan P Ashton
2412 S Summit
Sioux Falls SD 57105

Call Sign: KC0BBJ
Dale R Hochhalter
1106 S Summit Ave
Sioux Falls SD 57105

Call Sign: W0HSH
W Bruce Mc Leod
1600 S Summit Ave
Sioux Falls SD 57105

Call Sign: WD0GDF
Darrell R Seurer
3401 S Sundrop Ave
Sioux Falls SD 57110

Call Sign: KB0WSW
Anthony D Buss
705 S Tanglewood Ave
Sioux Falls SD 571068412

Call Sign: WA0UOS
Donald C Nelson
3205 S Terry
Sioux Falls SD 57106

Call Sign: WA0VMI
Mark W Nelson
3205 S Terry Ave
Sioux Falls SD 571061147

Call Sign: KC0LQR
Richard E Damian
5800 S Tomar Rd
Sioux Falls SD 57108

Call Sign: KC0EVS
Paul J De Boer
1907 S Walts
Sioux Falls SD 57105

Call Sign: KB0AUG
Jerry A Hiebert
708 S Walts Ave
Sioux Falls SD 571044745

Call Sign: KC0CHZ
Kevin W Sigl
3000 S Walts Ave
Sioux Falls SD 57105

Call Sign: KG9GG
George Pope
3101 S Walts Ave
Sioux Falls SD 57105

Call Sign: KD0QVF
R James Holmes
3101 S Walts Ave
Sioux Falls SD 57105

Call Sign: WD0FZW
Kelly C Hansen
405 S Walts Ave Apt 1
Sioux Falls SD 57104

Call Sign: W0CJM
Charles J Miller
7205 S Waterstone Cir
Sioux Falls SD 57108

Call Sign: N0PRJ
Dan W Lehmann
2205 S Wayland Ave
Sioux Falls SD 57105

Call Sign: N6SLN
Kevin D Ballenger
516 S Western Ave
Sioux Falls SD 571043927

Call Sign: WD0GNE
George Lair
1832 S Western Ave
Sioux Falls SD 57105

Call Sign: AB0I
Al Bolger
3700 S Westport 632
Sioux Falls SD 57106

Call Sign: K6ULB
Richard C Masterson Dds
3700 S Westport Av
Sioux Falls SD 571066360

Call Sign: N8ZOT
Claudia L Shanks
3700 S Westport Av 1071
Sioux Falls SD 571066344

Call Sign: WF8L
Bruce E Shanks
3700 S Westport Av 1071
Sioux Falls SD 571066344

Call Sign: KC3OK
John E Mc Carty
3700 S Westport Ave
Sioux Falls SD 57106

Call Sign: WB2RUU
Neil A Cinege
3700 S Westport Ave 1410
Sioux Falls SD 571066360

Call Sign: AB1L
Richard J Whelan
3700 S Westport Ave 1977
Sioux Falls SD 57106

Call Sign: N0DXO
Philip W Nelson
3700 S Westport Ave 1011
Sioux Falls SD 57106

Call Sign: KB2JSL
John D Armitage Jr
3700 S Westport Ave 1028
Sioux Falls SD 571066344

Call Sign: K7HG
John K Agrelius
3700 S Westport Ave 1059
Sioux Falls SD 57106

Call Sign: KC0SPK
Loyce M Taylor
3700 S Westport Ave 1087
Sioux Falls SD 57106

Call Sign: AC2J
Larry C Taylor
3700 S Westport Ave 1087
Sioux Falls SD 571066344

Call Sign: KC0VTQ
Raymond N Hansen
3700 S Westport Ave 1340
Sioux Falls SD 57106

Call Sign: KD0OXP
Charles A Newman
3700 S Westport Ave 1343
Sioux Falls SD 57106

Call Sign: AC0WU
Charles A Newman
3700 S Westport Ave 1343
Sioux Falls SD 57106

Call Sign: NF0K
Charles A Newman
3700 S Westport Ave 1343
Sioux Falls SD 57106

Call Sign: KD0PBS
Sherman W Conrow
370 S Westport Ave 1382
Sioux Falls SD 57106

Call Sign: NM5B
Bruce A Bowman
3700 S Westport Ave 1424
Sioux Falls SD 571066360

Call Sign: K5CMB
Celia M Bowman
3700 S Westport Ave 1424
Sioux Falls SD 571066360

Call Sign: WB0LRT
Harold D Ward
3700 S Westport Ave 1569
Sioux Falls SD 571066360

Call Sign: KC0PAB
Stanley F Vincent
3700 S Westport Ave 1587
Sioux Falls SD 57106

Call Sign: N0EBI
Elsie E Nelson
3700 S Westport Ave 1611
Sioux Falls SD 57106

Call Sign: KB7STH
Alice E Clark
3700 S Westport Ave 1646
Sioux Falls SD 571066360

Call Sign: KB7CCL
John A Clark
3700 S Westport Ave 1646
Sioux Falls SD 571066360

Call Sign: N8JMQ
Russell C Terjung
3700 S Westport Ave 1670
Sioux Falls SD 571066344

Call Sign: KD0CJX
Donald E Johnson
3700 S Westport Ave 1679
Sioux Falls SD 57106

Call Sign: W7DEJ
Donald E Johnson
3700 S Westport Ave 1679
Sioux Falls SD 57106

Call Sign: KC0TDB
Clyde R Clark Jr
3700 S Westport Ave 1939
Sioux Falls SD 57106

Call Sign: K0SKP
Clyde R Clark Jr
3700 S Westport Ave 1939
Sioux Falls SD 57106

Call Sign: AE4EW
Terrance V Vlug
3700 S Westport Ave 1994
Sioux Falls SD 57106

Call Sign: KD0IBG
Richard E Carpenter
3700 S Westport Ave 2072
Sioux Falls SD 57106

Call Sign: KF6NSU
Donald L Schleuse
3700 S Westport Ave 2087
Sioux Falls SD 57106

Call Sign: K1CGT
Thomas L Ferrari
3700 S Westport Ave 2148
Sioux Falls SD 57106

Call Sign: KA0VBG
Lois J Maas
3700 S Westport Ave 2242
Sioux Falls SD 571066360

Call Sign: W0HM
Herbert A Maas
3700 S Westport Ave 2242
Sioux Falls SD 571066360

Call Sign: KD0EOD
Robert H Paganelli
3700 S Westport Ave 2470
Sioux Falls SD 57106

Call Sign: KD0LQF
Suzanne Q Paganelli
3700 S Westport Ave 2470
Sioux Falls SD 57106

Call Sign: KD0MJE
Rudolph C Morris
3700 S Westport Ave 2500
Sioux Falls SD 57106

Call Sign: K1FDH
Rudolph C Morris
3700 S Westport Ave 2500
Sioux Falls SD 57106

Call Sign: W6DSB
Boyd L Fulbright Jr
3700 S Westport Ave 2502
Sioux Falls SD 571066360

Call Sign: N7KDW
Willard D Bass
3700 S Westport Ave 2617
Sioux Falls SD 57106

Call Sign: N0USO
Mary E Flinsbaugh
3700 S Westport Ave 2649
Sioux Falls SD 57106

Call Sign: N0SKV
George W Flinsbaugh
3700 S Westport Ave 2649
Sioux Falls SD 57106

Call Sign: N4ODT
Patricia O Mc Fall
3700 S Westport Ave 2654
Sioux Falls SD 57106

Call Sign: WB4PDO
Norman L Mc Fall
3700 S Westport Ave 2654
Sioux Falls SD 57106

Call Sign: K7GTF
Gregory T Faure
3700 S Westport Ave 2655
Sioux Falls SD 57106

Call Sign: W2ODH
James E Sharlow
3700 S Westport Ave 2675
Sioux Falls SD 57106

Call Sign: WA2ODH
Gayle A Sharlow
3700 S Westport Ave 2675
Sioux Falls SD 57106

Call Sign: N6WFN
Berte W Francisco
3700 S Westport Ave 2831
Sioux Falls SD 57106

Call Sign: KC0TTD
James E Staudacher
3700 S Westport Ave 2862
Sioux Falls SD 57106

Call Sign: KW7W
Ronald S Rose
3700 S Westport Ave 2921
Sioux Falls SD 57106

Call Sign: K6IMZ
Paul S Rumford
3700 S Westport Ave 2971
Sioux Falls SD 57106

Call Sign: KC0VTP
Donald J Bogle
3700 S Westport Ave 3044
Sioux Falls SD 57106

Call Sign: WD0BOG
Donald J Bogle
3700 S Westport Ave 3044
Sioux Falls SD 57106

Call Sign: WB5ODX
Russell F Smith
3700 S Westport Ave 3114
Sioux Falls SD 571066360

Call Sign: WD5FKM
Karen J Smith
3700 S Westport Ave 3114
Sioux Falls SD 571066360

Call Sign: KD0CXF
Robert C Stewart Jr
3700 S Westport Ave 3232
Sioux Falls SD 57106

Call Sign: WD0GIL
Raymond E Fink
3700 S Westport Ave 3288
Sioux Falls SD 571066360

Call Sign: K0VPR
George E Jensen
3700 S Westport Ave 3408
Sioux Falls SD 57106

Call Sign: N1YMG
Charles H Mc Crillis
3700 S Westport Ave 3463
Sioux Falls SD 571066360

Call Sign: WB0RED
Nelson C Lansdown
3700 S Westport Ave 3486
Sioux Falls SD 57106

Call Sign: WA5NMR
Nelson C Lansdown
3700 S Westport Ave 3486
Sioux Falls SD 57106

Call Sign: WA6HOR
Tom T Klemesrud
3700 S Westport Ave 3499
Sioux Falls SD 571066360

Call Sign: KL7JIE
Timothy H Coski
3700 S Westport Ave 3638
Sioux Falls SD 57106

Call Sign: W0ZOO
Joseph C Mulcahy
3700 S Westport Ave 3640
Sioux Falls SD 57106

Call Sign: KD6FHP
William R Evans
3700 S Westport Ave 368
Sioux Falls SD 57106

Call Sign: KD0QDQ
Byron O Howell
3700 S Westport Ave 3738
Sioux Falls SD 57106

Call Sign: KB2SGF
Kenneth M Anderson
3700 S Westport Ave 3802
Sioux Falls SD 571066360

Call Sign: KB2SGG
Annette E Anderson
3700 S Westport Ave 3802
Sioux Falls SD 571066360

Call Sign: KD0QXJ
Peter J Neubauer
3700 S Westport Ave 3851
Sioux Falls SD 57106

Call Sign: KE6QYT
Guy J Moppel
3700 S Westport Ave 3966
Sioux Falls SD 571066360

Call Sign: W0NJ
Merlin Loudenburg
3700 S Westport Ave 4073
Sioux Falls SD 571066360

Call Sign: KB7MUL
James Fausser
3700 S Westport Ave 41
Sioux Falls SD 57106

Call Sign: KB0ZPG
James R Tilton
3700 S Westport Ave 429
Sioux Falls SD 571066344

Call Sign: AA0RI
Charles E Carter
3700 S Westport Ave 44
Sioux Falls SD 571066360

Call Sign: KC0ZGD
Grace A Carter
3700 S Westport Ave 44
Sioux Falls SD 571066360

Call Sign: N0GAC
Grace A Carter
3700 S Westport Ave 44
Sioux Falls SD 571066360

Call Sign: KC0QGJ
Mary A Wilkinson
3700 S Westport Ave 490
Sioux Falls SD 57106

Call Sign: KC0QGI
Robert A Rechsteiner
3700 S Westport Ave 490
Sioux Falls SD 57106

Call Sign: KD0API
Martin Mcgaffey
3700 S Westport Ave 527
Sioux Falls SD 57106

Call Sign: KE6KNO
Charlotte L Schaefer
3700 S Westport Ave 551
Sioux Falls SD 57106

Call Sign: WB7DRB
Frank J Schaefer
3700 S Westport Ave 551
Sioux Falls SD 57106

Call Sign: KC5NVX
Mike E Camp
3700 S Westport Ave 596
Sioux Falls SD 57106

Call Sign: KC0QCQ
Donald W Douglas
3700 S Westport Ave 601
Sioux Falls SD 571056360

Call Sign: K6BOB
Robert S Lavin
3700 S Westport Ave 61
Sioux Falls SD 57106

Call Sign: KD0MNW
William B Amos
3700 S Westport Ave 612
Sioux Falls SD 57106

Call Sign: KC0QKH
Susan M Cole
3700 S Westport Ave 657
Sioux Falls SD 57106

Call Sign: W2KHU
Timothy Davis
3700 S Westport Ave 689
Sioux Falls SD 57106

Call Sign: KC0WJX
Robert P Martin
3700 S Westport Ave 739
Sioux Falls SD 57106

Call Sign: WA4CGG
John E Bryson III
3700 S Westport Ave 782
Sioux Falls SD 57106

Call Sign: WB6RSF
Robert E Nagels
3700 S Westport Ave 828
Sioux Falls SD 571066360

Call Sign: N5NIV
David E Harrison
3700 S Westport Ave 890
Sioux Falls SD 57106

Call Sign: KA0VST
Robert M Plain
3700 S Westport Ave 90
Sioux Falls SD 57106

Call Sign: KB1LON
David A Holt
3700 S Westport Ave 931
Sioux Falls SD 57106

Call Sign: AI8Q
Sue E Hagedon
3700 S Westport Ave 978
Sioux Falls SD 571066360

Call Sign: K1FDH
Rudolph C Morris
3700 S Westport Ave N 2500
Sioux Falls SD 57106

Call Sign: N8SFB
Carolyn R Morris
3700 S Westport Ave N 2500
Sioux Falls SD 57106

Call Sign: KI8IW
Gilbert O Styles
3700 S Westport Ave N 3744
Sioux Falls SD 57106

Call Sign: KG4NFO
Lemuel E Gatewood
3700 S Westport Ave Pmb 1195
Sioux Falls SD 57106

Call Sign: WB1AGA
William R Tamm
3700 S Westport Ave Pmb 3045
Sioux Falls SD 57106

Call Sign: KE6WUN
Barbara A Evans
3700 S Westport Ave Pmb 368
Sioux Falls SD 57106

Call Sign: AE8R
James M Hagedon Jr
3700 S Westport Ave Pmb 978
Sioux Falls SD 571066360

Call Sign: KF6LGN
Michael Anderson
5527 S Wexford Ct
Sioux Falls SD 57106

Call Sign: W0DPV
Michael R Koch
4001 S Woodwind Lane
Sioux Falls SD 57103

Call Sign: N0AEC
Myron R Wachendorf
2304 Southeastern Ave
Sioux Falls SD 57103

Call Sign: WA0JCV
Gerald L Van Loh
26979 Southeastern Ave
Sioux Falls SD 57108

Call Sign: KA0EMQ
Robert G Ensz
1016 Southwestern
Sioux Falls SD 57105

Call Sign: N0EWC
Valla Vee Dunn
1213 Sunny View Dr
Sioux Falls SD 571103004

Call Sign: WB0JYB
George E Dunn
1213 Sunny View Dr
Sioux Falls SD 571103004

Call Sign: N0XJC
Stephen F Park
3700 SW Port Ave Pmb 2235
Sioux Falls SD 57106

Call Sign: N9BTS
Daryl W Kraft
4213 Teakwood Ave
Sioux Falls SD 57103

Call Sign: KA0RHK
Todd D Gunn
5208 Thurman Dr
Sioux Falls SD 57106

Call Sign: KB0YVU
Andrew J Gunn
5208 Thurman Dr
Sioux Falls SD 57106

Call Sign: WA0CPW
Robert W Jensen
5009 Twin Ridge Rd
Sioux Falls SD 57106

Call Sign: N0PHC
Larry D Springer Jr
707 W 12th St
Sioux Falls SD 57104

Call Sign: WB0DAH
Anthony J Reeves
111 W 12th St 12
Sioux Falls SD 57102

Call Sign: KD0FZD
Harley L Waagmeester Jr
1712 W 12th St 16
Sioux Falls SD 57104

Call Sign: W0ROX
Harley L Waagmeester Jr
1712 W 12th St 16
Sioux Falls SD 57104

Call Sign: WA0SHA
Ross W Weber
717 W 13th St
Sioux Falls SD 57104

Call Sign: KD0DLX
Clyde D Price
621 W 13th St
Sioux Falls SD 57104

Call Sign: KC0ZSN
Rondi A Utne
923 W 15th St
Sioux Falls SD 57104

Call Sign: W0HWS
Willard A Coder
518 W 16th
Sioux Falls SD 57104

Call Sign: KD0NZJ
Terrill J Mcginley Sr
412 W 16th St Apt 6
Sioux Falls SD 57104

Call Sign: W0JLI
Harold K Lindseth
101 W 18 St 7
Sioux Falls SD 57105

Call Sign: WA0YRH
Diane D Belk
220 W 21st 1
Sioux Falls SD 57105

Call Sign: N0TFA
Matthew A Frederickson
220 W 21st St Apt 1
Sioux Falls SD 57105

Call Sign: KC0UDE
Michael C Digiulio
2609 W 26th St
Sioux Falls SD 57105

Call Sign: W0ZWH
Lawrence S Martin
1716 W 28 St
Sioux Falls SD 57105

Call Sign: WB0VUB
David A Viste
1500 W 30th
Sioux Falls SD 57105

Call Sign: KB0JJQ
Keith A Stoakes
406 W 30th St
Sioux Falls SD 57105

Call Sign: WB0CRP
Harold O Bailey
407 W 30th St
Sioux Falls SD 57105

Call Sign: WB0YMG
Elizabeth A Viste
1500 W 30th St
Sioux Falls SD 57105

Call Sign: WB0YUX
Solveig A Viste
1500 W 30th St
Sioux Falls SD 57105

Call Sign: WB0ZXQ
Mark E Viste
1500 W 30th St
Sioux Falls SD 57105

Call Sign: WB0VAL
Arlen E Viste
1500 W 30th St
Sioux Falls SD 571053622

Call Sign: KB0MCZ
Tom J Senden
1412 W 31st St
Sioux Falls SD 57105

Call Sign: KC0SEY
Brian J Fletcher
5408 W 31st St
Sioux Falls SD 57106

Call Sign: KG6IXW
Curtis R Cochran
5605 W 31st St
Sioux Falls SD 57106

Call Sign: K0WPC
Wesley J Tschetter
6500 W 32nd St
Sioux Falls SD 57106

Call Sign: N0HJH
Elaine Tschetter
6500 W 32nd St
Sioux Falls SD 57106

Call Sign: KC0DAS
William J Spreitzer
304 W 34th St
Sioux Falls SD 57105

Call Sign: WB0HAT
Randal G Sorenson
5817 W 35th St
Sioux Falls SD 57106

Call Sign: N0OLD
Judith A Lebakken
306 W 36th St 17
Sioux Falls SD 57105

Call Sign: W0GKU
Iris U Boyd
1609 W 38th St
Sioux Falls SD 57105

Call Sign: N0HRO
Pierce O Hanson
6001 W 40th St
Sioux Falls SD 57106

Call Sign: KB0IKW
Franklin J Murray
5909 W 41 St
Sioux Falls SD 57106

Call Sign: K0MCM
Brian E Ward
2522 W 41st St 186
Sioux Falls SD 57105

Call Sign: W0MCM
Veronica A Ward
2522 W 41st St 186
Sioux Falls SD 57105

Call Sign: K0VD
Naqro Club
2522 W 41st St 384
Sioux Falls SD 571056120

Call Sign: K0DD
Robert B Bonner
2522 W 41st St 384
Sioux Falls SD 571056120

Call Sign: KC0BHQ
Eric J Duwenhoegger
5001 W 43rd Apt 2
Sioux Falls SD 57106

Call Sign: N0GFK
Shawn B Pope
6010 W 43rd Apt 207
Sioux Falls SD 57106

Call Sign: KD0NBY
Jim R Dehoogh
6413 W 43rd St
Sioux Falls SD 57106

Call Sign: K9IEM
Luella Rayman
5001 W 45th St
Sioux Falls SD 57106

Call Sign: NS6U
George R Cosby Sr
5101 W 45th St 8
Sioux Falls SD 571061476

Call Sign: KA6NPC
Joyce D Cosby
5101 W 45th St Apt 8
Sioux Falls SD 57106

Call Sign: WB0YQS
Thomas E Davis
5505 W 46th St
Sioux Falls SD 57106

Call Sign: K0HKL
Keith L Halverson
4905 W 47th St
Sioux Falls SD 57106

Call Sign: KA0SDV
Terrance J Schulte
6704 W 47th St
Sioux Falls SD 57106

Call Sign: KF0MK
Linda K Purkapile
5212 W 47th St
Sioux Falls SD 571010867

Call Sign: WA5NDN
Brent J Clark
7308 W 51st St
Sioux Falls SD 57106

Call Sign: WB0YTY
Michael J Colburn
6425 W 56th St
Sioux Falls SD 57106

Call Sign: K0DFH
Michael J Colburn
6425 W 56th St
Sioux Falls SD 57106

Call Sign: KC0RWW
Walter R Koch
3800 W 71st St
Sioux Falls SD 57108

Call Sign: N0RFZ
Christopher C Meyer
2801 W 84th St N
Sioux Falls SD 571071115

Call Sign: KC0RDV
Brian G Matherly
848 W 8th St
Sioux Falls SD 57104

Call Sign: WB0RMD
Lyle K Lauck
6505 W 9th St
Sioux Falls SD 57107

Call Sign: KA0BRL
Morgan G Sarges
732 W 9th St Apt 2
Sioux Falls SD 57104

Call Sign: KB0PLB
Carol J Perry
4516 W Antelope Dr
Sioux Falls SD 57107

Call Sign: AA0NO
Steve E Perry
4516 W Antelope Dr
Sioux Falls SD 57107

Call Sign: KC0YHD
Thane K Williams
2500 W Bailey St
Sioux Falls SD 57104

Call Sign: KB0RHZ
Dianne P Enga
6300 W Benson Rd
Sioux Falls SD 57107

Call Sign: KB0WOE
Kevin C Enga
6300 W Benson Rd
Sioux Falls SD 57107

Call Sign: WB0PBI
Wallace N Enga
6300 W Benson Rd
Sioux Falls SD 57107

Call Sign: K0HAT
Dianne P Enga
6300 W Benson Rd
Sioux Falls SD 57107

Call Sign: W0RVE
Wallace N Enga
6300 W Benson Rd
Sioux Falls SD 57107

Call Sign: KC0TJO
Steven W Cook
3311 W Bitterroot St
Sioux Falls SD 57108

Call Sign: KB0MDA
James B Stalzer
5909 W Bristol Dr
Sioux Falls SD 57106

Call Sign: WJ0S
James B Stalzer
5909 W Bristol Dr
Sioux Falls SD 57106

Call Sign: N0DNQ
Bruce L Heitman
5817 W Bristol Dr
Sioux Falls SD 57106

Call Sign: N0HEC
James W Parkin
2609 W Brookings St
Sioux Falls SD 57104

Call Sign: K8ICZ
Mark G Fetcenko
2916 W Cinnamon Cir
Sioux Falls SD 57108

Call Sign: KC0RXE
Harold E Shuckhart
5724 W Coughvan Ct
Sioux Falls SD 57106

Call Sign: W0RNH
Loren M Miller
4605 W Custer Ln 205
Sioux Falls SD 57106

Call Sign: WD0EYV
Constance M Schaub
5615 W Dardanella Rd
Sioux Falls SD 571063412

Call Sign: KD0OPJ
Jennifer M Laflin
3901 W Innovation St Apt 211
Sioux Falls SD 57107

Call Sign: N0NZP
John M Wilson
400 W Jolyn Dr
Sioux Falls SD 57108

Call Sign: NI0I
Thomas M Wilson
400 W Jolyn Dr
Sioux Falls SD 571083802

Call Sign: N0URL
Robert T Wilson
400 W Jolyn Dr
Sioux Falls SD 57108

Call Sign: KC0SSD
David S Hatt
7464 W Legacy Ct
Sioux Falls SD 57106

Call Sign: N0HIV
David S Hatt
7464 W Legacy Ct
Sioux Falls SD 57106

Call Sign: K0BSG
David S Hatt
7464 W Legacy Ct
Sioux Falls SD 57106

Call Sign: KD0JDY
Paul D Yanzick
4416 W Peacock Dr
Sioux Falls SD 57107

Call Sign: K0AAX
Paul D Yanzick
4416 W Peacock Dr
Sioux Falls SD 57107

Call Sign: KB0YBR
Bernard M Mc Menamy
1205 W Ralph Rogers Rd
Sioux Falls SD 57108

Call Sign: W9NLK
James L Smith
912 W Ruby Pl
Sioux Falls SD 57106

Call Sign: KD0BUE
Edward J Gowlovech
6715 W Snowberry Cir
Sioux Falls SD 57106

Call Sign: WB0GHL
Roger D Syverson
8601 W Stoney Creek St
Sioux Falls SD 57106

Call Sign: KB0NYX
Joe D Cormack
5303 W Summer Creek
Sioux Falls SD 57106

Call Sign: K7EXO
Stanley R Gunn
5305 W Sunnydale Pl
Sioux Falls SD 57106

Call Sign: KD0OKP
Christopher J Carlisle
1609 W Thora Cir
Sioux Falls SD 57108

Call Sign: W5GTL
Christopher J Carlisle
1609 W Thora Cir
Sioux Falls SD 57108

Call Sign: KD0OKQ
Gabe B Carlisle
1609 W Thora Cir
Sioux Falls SD 57108

Call Sign: KC0DAW
Troy M Schnetter
804 W Tradewinds St
Sioux Falls SD 57108

Call Sign: KB0WSV
Steven M Kittelsrud
3704 W Urban Cir
Sioux Falls SD 57108

Call Sign: KB0OJN
Mark P Henry
4407 W Valhalla Apt 9
Sioux Falls SD 57106

Call Sign: KD0BUF
Daniel P Smith
4403 W Valhalla Blvd Apt 18
Sioux Falls SD 57106

Call Sign: KC0OQE
John H Watson
3700 W Westport Ave 1508
Sioux Falls SD 57106

Call Sign: W0SKP
John H Watson
3700 W Westport Ave 1508
Sioux Falls SD 57106

Call Sign: WR9M
Robert B Stevens
West Port Ave 3750
Sioux Falls SD 57106

Call Sign: KE6YUH
Don Ortloff
Westport Ave 555
Sioux Falls SD 57106

Call Sign: KB0YEL
Nicolas E Rae
2337 Woodbine Ln
Sioux Falls SD 57103

Call Sign: KB9FTO
Jason P Heym
Sioux Falls SD 57186

Call Sign: KC0SSA
Sioux Empire Ares/Skywarn
Sioux Falls SD 57101

Call Sign: W0FSD
Sioux Empire Ares/Skywarn
Sioux Falls SD 57101

Call Sign: W0ZWY
Sioux Empire Amateur Radio Club
Sioux Falls SD 57101

Call Sign: WB0TML
Richard F Ballieu
Sioux Falls SD 57101

Call Sign: KD0QMN
Alan G Kingsley
Sioux Falls SD 57101

Call Sign: KB0QMH
Shannon M Cook
Sioux Falls SD 57109

Call Sign: KC0VDE

Brian E Ward
Sioux Falls SD 57109

Call Sign: KD0KUA
Veronica A Flemming
Sioux Falls SD 57109

Call Sign: KI0JW
Troy P Nusz
Sioux Falls SD 57118

Call Sign: KG6INO
Erik W Osterman
Sioux Falls SD 57186

Call Sign: KD0OXC
Christopher C Graves
Sioux Falls SD 57186

Call Sign: KC7KUP
Gregory J Feddema
Sioux Falls SD 571090713

Call Sign: KC0UDD
Gary Million
Sioux Falls SD 571098543

Call Sign: W0NTS
Dennis L Hoffman
Sioux Falls SD 571184256

Call Sign: N1JLV
Jonathann D Westerling
Sioux Falls SD 571860001

FCC Amateur Radio Licenses in Sisseton

Call Sign: W0WM
Percy A Aadland
111 4th Ave E
Sisseton SD 57262

Call Sign: KH7DI
Gregory A Kaahanui

605 5th Ave W
Sisseton SD 572621237

Call Sign: KF0MD
Jonathan R Green
302 Coteau Blvd
Sisseton SD 57262

Call Sign: KB0KGO
Matt B Johnson
RR1
Sisseton SD 57762

Call Sign: WA0IXJ
Douglas M Just
RR2
Sisseton SD 57262

Call Sign: KD0HK
Edwin P Hagen Jr
Rt 3
Sisseton SD 57262

Call Sign: N0EPP
Glen O Johnson
11609 Sica Hollow Rd 15
Sisseton SD 572629403

Call Sign: KB0KGP
Dustin L Thode
311 W Maple
Sisseton SD 57262

FCC Amateur Radio Licenses in Smithwick

Call Sign: KD0NYH
Leona B Fleming
Smithwick SD 57782

FCC Amateur Radio Licenses in Spearfish

Call Sign: KC0GKF
Ryan J Jennings

3308 12th Ave
Spearfish SD 57783

Call Sign: WD0AIP
Todd D Knutson
3109 7th Ave
Spearfish SD 57783

Call Sign: NI8X
Allan W Smail
1605 Arizona Ave
Spearfish SD 57783

Call Sign: WB0TBP
La Verne R Clark
603 E Colorado Blvd
Spearfish SD 57783

Call Sign: KC0OMS
Daryl W Alderman
703 E Grant St
Spearfish SD 57783

Call Sign: KB0NCB
Sharon G Stegner
640 E Hudson Apt 104
Spearfish SD 57783

Call Sign: KD0NAO
Marcus J Smith
340 E Kansas
Spearfish SD 57783

Call Sign: W0MZ
Marcus J Smith
340 E Kansas
Spearfish SD 57783

Call Sign: KB0TCL
Tom O Meyer
120 E Michigan
Spearfish SD 57783

Call Sign: KC0QYF
Sean N Donnelly

440 E Michigan
Spearfish SD 57783

Call Sign: N0HFG
Edward K Smith
639 E Michigan M4
Spearfish SD 57783

Call Sign: KC0PI
Richard W Ulmer
19682 Fish Lane
Spearfish SD 57783

Call Sign: KC0KFX
Lennard Hopper
111 Grandview Dr
Spearfish SD 57783

Call Sign: KW9L
Terrence D Pelkola
906 Heritage Dr
Spearfish SD 57783

Call Sign: N0YBK
Darlene K Telkamp
32 Horseshoe Ln
Spearfish SD 57783

Call Sign: K0RNT
Ray N Telkamp
32 Horseshoe Ln
Spearfish SD 577831128

Call Sign: KB0RPH
Benjamin A Burgeson
1875 Lookout Mountain Rd
Spearfish SD 57783

Call Sign: KD0BKP
John F Gunderson
18 Lourie Lane
Spearfish SD 57783

Call Sign: KB0POH
Aaron R Sachau

1316 Meadowlark Ct
Spearfish SD 57783

Call Sign: N0UCR
Michael J Headley
2110 Mustang Lane
Spearfish SD 57783

Call Sign: N0GRS
G Randy Sachau
1440 N 10th St
Spearfish SD 57783

Call Sign: KB0HRC
Kendall J Aldinger
2507 N 2nd St
Spearfish SD 57783

Call Sign: NU0E
Jay E Gorham
1444 N 3rd St
Spearfish SD 577831404

Call Sign: KE6WDF
Richard L J Crawford
507 N 3rd St Apt 1
Spearfish SD 57783

Call Sign: K0JV
Jerry K Van Vactor
1435 N 5th St
Spearfish SD 57783

Call Sign: W0ASZ
Terry M Anderson
810 N Main St 281
Spearfish SD 57783

Call Sign: AL7PF
Patricia A Daft
430 Oriol Dr G 43
Spearfish SD 57783

Call Sign: K6GZL
Robert H Weaver

3135 Ridge Rd
Spearfish SD 57783

Call Sign: K0GZL
Robert H Weaver
3135 Ridge Rd
Spearfish SD 577836024

Call Sign: W0TDK
Todd D Knutson
20073 Ridgefield Loop
Spearfish SD 57783

Call Sign: KC0GWT
Matthew R Loken
RR1
Spearfish SD 57783

Call Sign: KA0VGN
Scott C Nauman
117 S 5th St
Spearfish SD 57783

Call Sign: N0VMD
Alan W Wessel
1002 Spartan Dr
Spearfish SD 57783

Call Sign: KD0CEV
Joshua A Job
1919 Stampeade Dr
Spearfish SD 57783

Call Sign: K0HP
Donald J Matthesen
3125 Thorne Pl
Spearfish SD 57783

Call Sign: KB0ZXP
James I Meyer
227 Thunderbolt Ct
Spearfish SD 57783

Call Sign: KB0GZQ
Thomas E Secrest

101 Timberline
Spearfish SD 57783

Call Sign: KD0DDN
Thomas E Secrest
101 Timberline Rd
Spearfish SD 57783

Call Sign: KF0QB
Harry J Irwin
292 Upper Valley
Spearfish SD 57783

Call Sign: K0AS
Arne R Sjomeling Jr
292 Upper Valley Rd
Spearfish SD 57783

Call Sign: W0IG
Jene H Melton
100 Vale Rd
Spearfish SD 577831172

Call Sign: K0ZWX
Ralph R Noonan Sr
811 Verdale Dr
Spearfish SD 57783

Call Sign: KD0BLU
Spearfish Amateur Radio Club
10559 W Hwy 14
Spearfish SD 57783

Call Sign: KN3LSB
Spearfish Amateur Radio Club
10559 W Hwy 14
Spearfish SD 57783

Call Sign: KD7GLY
Joanna R Jones Ms
10559 W Hwy 14
Spearfish SD 57783

Call Sign: K7RE
Brian D Kassel

10559 W Hwy 14
Spearfish SD 577836603

Call Sign: WA0BDN
Larry D Miller
309 Yellowstone Pl
Spearfish SD 57783

Call Sign: WB0LIW
Graham H Chesnut
318 Yellowstone Pl
Spearfish SD 577832954

Call Sign: KB0YAJ
Everett E Burgeson
Spearfish SD 57783

FCC Amateur Radio Licenses in Spencer

Call Sign: N3SMR
Leslie E Zellers
723 Wilcox St
Spencer SD 573740256

FCC Amateur Radio Licenses in Springfield

Call Sign: KB0TZF
Patricia A Thomas
41146 314th St
Springfield SD 570626317

Call Sign: KB0NKB
William J Ferwerda
31362 407th Ave
Springfield SD 570626205

Call Sign: KC0GSR
Calvin D Dejong
31274 410 Ave
Springfield SD 57062

Call Sign: KC0IXV
Calvin D Dejong

31274 410 Ave
Springfield SD 57062

Call Sign: KA0WTY
Marilyn J Stone
512 8th St
Springfield SD 57062

Call Sign: KA0WTZ
Nelson C Stone
512 8th St
Springfield SD 57062

Call Sign: WP4ISH
Tracy G Guptill
41069 Hwy 37
Springfield SD 57062

Call Sign: KB0PGY
Tammy L Johnson-Dejong
31274 SD Hwy 37
Springfield SD 57062

Call Sign: WB0PWD
Calvin D Dejong
31274 SD Hwy 37
Springfield SD 57062

Call Sign: KB0VAF
Corey S Thomas
41146 SD Hwy 37
Springfield SD 570626317

Call Sign: KB0VAG
Brian N Thomas
41146 SD Hwy 37
Springfield SD 570626317

Call Sign: N0AYL
Raymond N Thomas
41146 SD Hwy 37
Springfield SD 570626317

Call Sign: KA0LLT
John C Kuckleburg

Springfield SD 57062

Call Sign: KA0MAZ
Judy M Kuckleburg
Springfield SD 57062

Call Sign: AA0VG
Gary D Guptill
Springfield SD 570620001

FCC Amateur Radio Licenses in Stephen

Call Sign: KC0MEE
Cameron J Crow
Stephen SD 57346

FCC Amateur Radio Licenses in Stickney

Call Sign: KC0CRI
Roy G Messing
418 Main St
Stickney SD 57375

Call Sign: KC0GRG
Tyler J Gerlach
Stickney SD 57375

FCC Amateur Radio Licenses in Stockholm

Call Sign: KC0YMV
Ronald E Marko
15446 468th Ave
Stockholm SD 57264

FCC Amateur Radio Licenses in Sturgis

Call Sign: N0MHJ
Eugene W Mc Pherson
1807 3rd St
Sturgis SD 57785

Call Sign: KC0CCB
Todd Rittel
408 7th St
Sturgis SD 57785

Call Sign: KC0PJN
John E Erickson
1040 Ball Park Rd G 15
Sturgis SD 57785

Call Sign: KC0FNE
Michael L Cruickshank
1060 Ballpark Rd Apt G18
Sturgis SD 57785

Call Sign: K0ODY
Rupert W Potter
8055 Blucksberg Dr
Sturgis SD 57785

Call Sign: KC0QYG
Arthur M Morris
8063 Blucksberg Dr
Sturgis SD 57785

Call Sign: WB0JEK
David A Mattox
21090 Cardinal Pl
Sturgis SD 57785

Call Sign: WB0KUE
Deloris L Rose
1220 Cedar St
Sturgis SD 57785

Call Sign: KC0TKN
Gary A Moore
2301 Colorado Dr
Sturgis SD 57785

Call Sign: KC0VZT
Christian L Stallkamp
121 David Dr
Sturgis SD 57785

Call Sign: WA0OVR
Donald E Ericson
710 Douglas St
Sturgis SD 57785

Call Sign: N0MAQ
Wade A Sheeder
919 Dudley St
Sturgis SD 57785

Call Sign: KD7NRG
Roy O Kornmeyer
2340 E Ave M10
Sturgis SD 57785

Call Sign: N0RBQ
Brent A Lyons
1916 Elk Rd
Sturgis SD 57785

Call Sign: N0XJM
Autumn D Lyons
1916 Elk Rd
Sturgis SD 57785

Call Sign: KC0TKO
Charles M Douvier
13891 Falcon Pl
Sturgis SD 57785

Call Sign: KA0EFT
Clifford W Meyer
HC 55
Sturgis SD 57785

Call Sign: N3PJG
Warren E Shaulis
2304 Holly Court 2
Sturgis SD 57785

Call Sign: N0DCM
Ray J Kuckleburg
2009 Lazelle St Apt A
Sturgis SD 57785

Call Sign: N7CLC
Cynthia L Collister
11918 Meadow Court
Sturgis SD 57785

Call Sign: KC0INJ
Troy M Sage
20530 N Merritt Pl
Sturgis SD 57785

Call Sign: N0HLL
Cheryl D Roth
7746 N Wild Turkey Dr
Sturgis SD 57785

Call Sign: W0LDS
Cheryl D Roth
7746 N Wild Turkey Dr
Sturgis SD 57785

Call Sign: KS0R
Randal L Roth
7746 N Wild Turkey Dr
Sturgis SD 577859602

Call Sign: N0OUS
Lenore E Hines
1300 Nellie
Sturgis SD 57785

Call Sign: N0AEL
Donald P Hines
1300 Nellie
Sturgis SD 577852053

Call Sign: KC7OZD
Ron D Roth
2307 S Fulton
Sturgis SD 57785

Call Sign: KB0NNT
Gerald D Majzner
14072 SD Hwy 34
Sturgis SD 57785

Call Sign: KD5AQH
John P Kellogg
740 Sherman St
Sturgis SD 57785

Call Sign: KA0EER
Vernon J Meyer
20788 Story Ln
Sturgis SD 57785

Call Sign: N0TBX
Daryl P Zimmerman
12165 Warren Loop
Sturgis SD 57785

FCC Amateur Radio Licenses in Summit

Call Sign: K0ZFI
Alfred W Redlin
RR1
Summit SD 57266

FCC Amateur Radio Licenses in Tabor

Call Sign: KC0TOW
Barry M Schloss
31071 Boy Scout Rd
Tabor SD 570636202

Call Sign: KC0BWQ
Vickie M Lammers
204 Hakl
Tabor SD 57063

Call Sign: KC0AXR
Kevin S Lammers
204 N Hakl
Tabor SD 57063

FCC Amateur Radio Licenses in Tea

Call Sign: KD0OKR

Scott P Bentz
240 Highpointe St Apt 56
Tea SD 57064

Call Sign: W0DNV
Homer F Anshutz
508 W 3rd St
Tea SD 570640653

Call Sign: W0ACT
Walter T Wichner
Tea SD 57064

Call Sign: KC0OVX
Carl L Bruce
Tea SD 57064

FCC Amateur Radio Licenses in Toronto

Call Sign: KC0OVC
Roland D Thompson
220 Missouri
Toronto SD 57268

FCC Amateur Radio Licenses in Trent

Call Sign: W0QT
Carl E Lamping
Rt 1
Trent SD 57065

Call Sign: KD0IYL
Kenneth L Albers
309 W 3rd St
Trent SD 57065

Call Sign: K0KLA
Kenneth L Albers
309 W 3rd St
Trent SD 57065

FCC Amateur Radio Licenses in Tripp

Call Sign: KF6WJG
Alan J Brenholt
202 N Henry St
Tripp SD 57376

Call Sign: WD0BXD
Twila L Jacobson
303 S Carpenter St
Tripp SD 57376

Call Sign: KA0DTT
Clinton Fuerst
101 S Hasset Box 417
Tripp SD 57376

Call Sign: N0SIC
Alvin M Roth
Tripp SD 57376

FCC Amateur Radio Licenses in Tyndall

Call Sign: N0OII
Alan L Nedved
41809 305th St
Tyndall SD 57066

Call Sign: KD0CZV
Richard L Nedved
41809 305th St
Tyndall SD 57066

Call Sign: N0OII
Richard L Nedved
41809 305th St
Tyndall SD 57066

Call Sign: KB0VPP
Joe A Plihal
Tyndall SD 57066

Call Sign: KC0ABT
Kim D Sage
Tyndall SD 57066

Call Sign: W0WH
Cletus Szymanski
Tyndall SD 57066

FCC Amateur Radio Licenses in Utica

Call Sign: N0RAL
Dean J Bierle
RR1
Utica SD 57067

Call Sign: KA0MDS
Gary L Diede
Utica SD 57067

FCC Amateur Radio Licenses in Valley Springs

Call Sign: KC0BOB
Gerald M Merkouris
26216 484th Ave
Valley Springs SD 57068

Call Sign: KC0CDE
Gary L Morinville
26465 484th Ave
Valley Springs SD 57068

Call Sign: KC0DAU
Maureen E Morinville
26465 484th Ave
Valley Springs SD 57068

Call Sign: KC0SSU
Luke J Comeau
918 Broadway Ave
Valley Springs SD 57068

Call Sign: KC0USR
Machelle A Comeau
918 Broadway Ave
Valley Springs SD 57068

Call Sign: W0DDN

Peter C De King Jr
411 Elm
Valley Springs SD 57068

FCC Amateur Radio Licenses in Vermillion

Call Sign: W0UD
Robert W Wood
46296 313th St
Vermillion SD 570699614

Call Sign: KC0LHP
Chris S Hans
425 Adams 69
Vermillion SD 57069

Call Sign: KA0ARC
Thomas E Vogel
401 Catalina
Vermillion SD 57069

Call Sign: N0ECX
Amy K Vogel
401 Catalina
Vermillion SD 57069

Call Sign: WA0WLA
Barbara W Hoag
826 Crawford Rd
Vermillion SD 57069

Call Sign: WS0B
Norman J Field
833 Duke St 83
Vermillion SD 57069

Call Sign: KE0PM
Michael E Mortensen
323 E Lewis
Vermillion SD 57069

Call Sign: KC0OGR
Kenneth W James
614 E Main

Vermillion SD 57069

Call Sign: KB0EMW
Wayne E Leibel
8 Evergreen
Vermillion SD 57069

Call Sign: N0YUJ
Robert A Boston
15 Franklin
Vermillion SD 57069

Call Sign: KB0CBY
Kemberli A Eveleth
209 Green St
Vermillion SD 57069

Call Sign: W0MMQ
Roy J Jorgensen
803 Lewis
Vermillion SD 57069

Call Sign: KD0BDR
Robert E Grossman
818 Madison St
Vermillion SD 57069

Call Sign: WA0NUU
Eugene G Hoag
826 N Crawford Rd
Vermillion SD 57069

Call Sign: AC0ZA
Scott A Yellig
N Dakota St
Vermillion SD 57069

Call Sign: N0EPY
Richard H Hammond
27 N Yale St
Vermillion SD 57069

Call Sign: N0IUB
Richard A Mc Bride
2102 Old Bridge Rd

Vermillion SD 570699776

Call Sign: W5VGI
Edward G Ezrailson
1301 Over Dr
Vermillion SD 57069

Call Sign: WB0PPS
Isaac Hoag
219 Prospect St
Vermillion SD 57069

Call Sign: KB0KPV
Tim C Cowman
913 Rice Dr
Vermillion SD 57069

Call Sign: N0ACN
Tim C Cowman
913 Rice Dr
Vermillion SD 57069

Call Sign: KC0VSI
Nick R Britten
1114 Ridgecrest Dr
Vermillion SD 57069

Call Sign: KB0DOZ
Richard J Piper
RR1
Vermillion SD 57069

Call Sign: K0MI
Michael W Marek
29 S Crawford Rd
Vermillion SD 57069

Call Sign: KA0UFI
Michael R Rumelhart
202 S Pine
Vermillion SD 57069

Call Sign: KC0SZU
David B Lewison
214 S Walker St

Vermillion SD 570693311

Call Sign: N0CMT
Marlene R Christensen
948 Sunset Dr
Vermillion SD 57069

Call Sign: KC4EGT
Ella F Williams
902 Valley View Dr
Vermillion SD 570693547

Call Sign: KC4EHY
Gerald G Williams
902 Valley View Dr
Vermillion SD 570693547

Call Sign: N0BPC
Clyde F Watts
916 W Main St
Vermillion SD 57069

Call Sign: WB7NMY
Timothy H Heaton
216 Willow St
Vermillion SD 57069

Call Sign: KA3NFX
Frank M Marshall
Vermillion SD 57069

Call Sign: N0HEU
Donald L Ziegler
Vermillion SD 57069

Call Sign: KR0T
Larry A Schuh
Vermillion SD 57069

Call Sign: W0VIM
Harry L Scholten
Vermillion SD 57069

FCC Amateur Radio Licenses in Viborg

Call Sign: WA0QLP
Thomas E Hill
28829 448th Ave
Viborg SD 57070

Call Sign: W0OOZ
Shirley A Leih
103 Clark
Viborg SD 570700523

Call Sign: KD0NZL
Matthew L Schooley
Viborg SD 57070

FCC Amateur Radio Licenses in Virgil

Call Sign: W0BHP
Hazel I Curtis
RR1
Virgil SD 57379

Call Sign: W0VQC
Frank L Curtis Jr
RR1
Virgil SD 57379

Call Sign: W0VHB
Carol J Gildemaster
Rt 1
Virgil SD 57379

FCC Amateur Radio Licenses in Volga

Call Sign: KB0ZWV
Steven P Schwartz
524 Astrachan Ave
Volga SD 57071

Call Sign: WA0AIL
Eugene Cotton
E
Volga SD 57071

Call Sign: N0VEK
Kurt C Narveson
315 Hansina Ave
Volga SD 57071

Call Sign: N0ZMJ
Cathy L Narveson
315 Hansina Ave
Volga SD 57071

Call Sign: N0YVP
Eileen M Schnell
703 Kasan Ave
Volga SD 57071

Call Sign: KA0NPW
Gregory E Moir
503 Lincoln Ln
Volga SD 57071

Call Sign: N0XQE
Phyllis K Moir
503 Lincoln Ln
Volga SD 57071

Call Sign: WA0OMK
John A Tevedahl
Rfd 1
Volga SD 57071

Call Sign: N0JJX
Warren D Aman
Volga SD 57071

Call Sign: KD0MSW
Tyler D Gross
Volga SD 57071

Call Sign: KB0QEE
Nancy A Anderson
21413 460th Ave
Volya SD 57071

Call Sign: KB0AJJ
Paul K Kruse
Wagner SD 57380

Call Sign: KI6ROB
Robert M Silvano
30367 SD Hwy 19
Wakonda SD 57073

Call Sign: KC9CGQ
Matthew Burtz
213 2nd Ave
Wall SD 57790

Call Sign: N0ZLP
David M Federwitz
Wall SD 57790

Call Sign: N0GHM
Arnold B Wibeto
15472 437th Ave
Wallace SD 57272

Call Sign: N0GHN
Dorothy M Wibeto
15472 437th Ave
Wallace SD 57272

Call Sign: AA0BB
Eldon J Jameson
Wallace SD 57272

Call Sign: N0GKZ

Merle A Kolden
Wallace SD 57272

FCC Amateur Radio Licenses in Warner

Call Sign: KB0JHR
J R Arlt
23 1st St NE
Warner SD 57479

Call Sign: N0IQX
D J Adams
Warner SD 57479

Call Sign: N0MPY
Jane K Adams
Warner SD 57479

Call Sign: KD0HUI
Michael J Goetz
Warner SD 57479

Call Sign: KD0EFI
Rieck J Eske
Warner SD 57479

Call Sign: KD0NIK
Wayde L Schwarting
Warner SD 57479

FCC Amateur Radio Licenses in Watertown

Call Sign: W0IT
Stanley L Burghardt
315 10th Ave NW
Watertown SD 57201

Call Sign: KC0VHY
Ryan C Killion
412 10th St SE
Watertown SD 57201

Call Sign: KC0DWY

Chad S Sandue
2002 11th Ave SW
Watertown SD 57201

Call Sign: KF0HL
Dennis G Warrick
1348 12th St NE
Watertown SD 572018002

Call Sign: KC0LRV
George A Slama
1372 12th St NE
Watertown SD 572018002

Call Sign: KB0GMU
Ruth Archer
12th St NW
Watertown SD 57201

Call Sign: KB0NQH
Victor J Yexley
2400 13th Ave SW
Watertown SD 572017199

Call Sign: KC0OVD
Debra L Richardson
1015 13th St NE
Watertown SD 57201

Call Sign: KC0ODQ
Jeffery L Richardson
1015 13th St NE
Watertown SD 57201

Call Sign: KC0PLY
Melissa L Richardson
1015 13th St NE
Watertown SD 57201

Call Sign: KC0TLT
Jason W Ploff
1838 14th Ave SE
Watertown SD 57201

Call Sign: KC0VFX

Vicky L Ploof
1838 14th Ave SE
Watertown SD 57201

Call Sign: KC0PLX
Timothy B Leveque
1839 14th Ave SE
Watertown SD 57201

Call Sign: KC0TLS
Tracy L Leveque
1839 14th Ave SE
Watertown SD 57201

Call Sign: KD0LJH
John A Birnell
3210 15th Ave SW
Watertown SD 57201

Call Sign: KB0KFI
Bryan A Tierney
19 15th St SE
Watertown SD 57201

Call Sign: KB0LCR
Kevin M Harrington
45243 174 St
Watertown SD 57201

Call Sign: KC0YQC
Jean M Cherland
45243 174th St
Watertown SD 57201

Call Sign: KC0PMZ
Roger E Maine
5 17th Ave SW
Watertown SD 57201

Call Sign: WD8DVI
Paul H Van Gorkom
126 17th St NE
Watertown SD 572012924

Call Sign: KB0KBH

Skeet T Skaalen
511 17th St NE
Watertown SD 57201

Call Sign: WB0ZQT
Donald D Hegg
1105 17th St NE
Watertown SD 57201

Call Sign: KC0MYT
Jeff D Moore
112 18 St NW
Watertown SD 57201

Call Sign: KD0NIQ
Meghan E Olson
1st Ave SE
Watertown SD 57201

Call Sign: KC0TCM
Janelle B Nygaard
403 20th Ave NW
Watertown SD 57201

Call Sign: N0JH
Darwin J Hegg
4102 20th Ave SW
Watertown SD 572017034

Call Sign: KD0HWL
Byron I Callies Sr
1332 20th St NE
Watertown SD 57201

Call Sign: WB0MRS
James A Redlin
218 21st St SW
Watertown SD 57201

Call Sign: KC0YQD
Jon M Bargmann
1105 24th St SW
Watertown SD 57201

Call Sign: KC0MYV

Michele L Engels
1052 29th St SE
Watertown SD 57201

Call Sign: N0XKP
Harry A Johnson
710 2nd Ave NE
Watertown SD 57201

Call Sign: KB0GNA
Minoru Tsukamoto
115 2nd Ave SE
Watertown SD 57201

Call Sign: N0MDQ
Vincent L Archer
215 2nd Ave SE
Watertown SD 57201

Call Sign: KB9HLY
De Orval B Purintun
1114 2nd Ave SE
Watertown SD 57201

Call Sign: N0FXX
Forrest J Tassler
1119 2nd Ave SE
Watertown SD 57201

Call Sign: KB0IOW
Martin C Geffre
1227 2nd Ave SE
Watertown SD 57201

Call Sign: KB0GXR
Alvin E Meisenheimer
214 2nd Ave SW
Watertown SD 57201

Call Sign: N0YGU
Michael P Riter
321 2nd St
Watertown SD 57201

Call Sign: KB0RBG

Clark J Adams
409 2nd St NE
Watertown SD 57201

Call Sign: KB0WJL
Eric J Adams
409 2nd St NE
Watertown SD 57201

Call Sign: W0SDH
Donald P Egert
1133 2nd St NW
Watertown SD 57201

Call Sign: N0XKO
Steven J Stydel
1341 2nd St NW
Watertown SD 57201

Call Sign: WA0SBT
Mylo C Andersen
721 3rd Ave NW
Watertown SD 57201

Call Sign: W6DNY
Greg S Smith
1503 3rd Ave NW
Watertown SD 57201

Call Sign: N0GHL
David D Hegg
710 3rd St NE
Watertown SD 57201

Call Sign: KB8HMR
Laurel A Foss
1167 3rd St NW
Watertown SD 57201

Call Sign: N0RMQ
Terri D Grey
310 3rd St SE
Watertown SD 57201

Call Sign: KG0UR

Wesley P Smith
1112 43rd St NW
Watertown SD 57201

Call Sign: KB0IUR
John W Jackson
1122 43rd St NW
Watertown SD 57201

Call Sign: KB5VLE
Terri A Mayfield
17296 447th Ave
Watertown SD 57201

Call Sign: KK0SD
Gary J Mayfield
17296 447th Ave
Watertown SD 57201

Call Sign: KC0MYU
Sarah A Smith
16180 453 Ave
Watertown SD 57201

Call Sign: N0TAF
James A Pond
16725 459th Ave
Watertown SD 57201

Call Sign: KB0KBI
James J Sumner
1174 4th St NW
Watertown SD 57201

Call Sign: KB0NOG
Rachel A Engel
1240 4th St NW
Watertown SD 57201

Call Sign: NT0Q
Kurt D Engel
1240 4th St NW
Watertown SD 57201

Call Sign: KC0NLM

Elizabeth D Engel
1240 4th St NW
Watertown SD 57201

Call Sign: KC0YPZ
Dwn M Engel
1240 4th St NW
Watertown SD 57201

Call Sign: WA0KDM
William E Johnson
423 4th St SE
Watertown SD 57201

Call Sign: KB0AJZ
Kelly J Hawkinson
1115 5th Ave NE
Watertown SD 572011904

Call Sign: N0HFH
Daniel L Hawkinson
1115 5th Ave NE
Watertown SD 572011904

Call Sign: KC0LRT
Robert A Campbell
1119 5th Ave SE
Watertown SD 57201

Call Sign: K0ZBJ
Robert L Hoaas Sr
336 6th St
Watertown SD 57201

Call Sign: KC0YPY
Adam J Renner
203 6th St NE
Watertown SD 57201

Call Sign: KB0OEO
Scott D Brown
318 6th St NE
Watertown SD 57201

Call Sign: KS5Z

Gary J Mayfield
1908 6th St NE
Watertown SD 57201

Call Sign: WD0FKC
Timothy A Moes
320 7th St NE
Watertown SD 57201

Call Sign: KB0GMY
Vicki E Rehder
713 7th St NE
Watertown SD 57201

Call Sign: K0JNH
John N Hauff
203 8 St SW
Watertown SD 572013336

Call Sign: KB0NOE
Wendell L Lunde
308 8St NE
Watertown SD 57201

Call Sign: KA0SNM
Ross B Lindgren
22 8th Ave SW 311
Watertown SD 57201

Call Sign: KC0FTM
Michael J Smith
1709 B Ave
Watertown SD 57102

Call Sign: KC0NLN
Nuttaphon Ungnapatanin
2030 Birch Ave
Watertown SD 57201

Call Sign: WB0VAR
Robert F Rousseau
1184 Crestview Dr
Watertown SD 57201

Call Sign: KC0TKX

Christian D Oien
19 E Highland Blvd
Watertown SD 57201

Call Sign: KC0YQA
David C Harrington
1020 E Kemp
Watertown SD 57201

Call Sign: WB0WIH
James A Stinson
1211 E Kemp
Watertown SD 57201

Call Sign: KC0MYS
Troy A Cordell
E Kemp Apt B
Watertown SD 57201

Call Sign: WB0YCM
Karl O Bates
1234 E Kemp Ave
Watertown SD 57201

Call Sign: KC0TCL
Jared K Sogn
1606 Grandview Dr
Watertown SD 57201

Call Sign: WD4RDQ
Geraldine F Crocker
1123 Lincoln Ave NE
Watertown SD 572017397

Call Sign: WD4RDR
Darrel G Crocker
1123 Lincoln Ave NE
Watertown SD 572017397

Call Sign: KC0YQB
Sabina K Pathan
44761 Lyle Lake Rd
Watertown SD 57235

Call Sign: W6IVV

Glenn R Edland
1170 Mayfair
Watertown SD 57201

Call Sign: KC0MNO
Chad J Koistinen
1115 Mayfair Dr
Watertown SD 57201

Call Sign: W0LPG
Valgene E Alwin
1148 N Broadway
Watertown SD 572011227

Call Sign: W0MBF
Richard W Egert
494 N Lake Dr
Watertown SD 57201

Call Sign: KA0IAL
Robert J Burkine
1845 N Westminster 115
Watertown SD 57201

Call Sign: KD0RHS
Gary A Ebner
624 S Broadway
Watertown SD 57201

Call Sign: N0KXE
Larry R Boyer
382 S Lake Dr
Watertown SD 57201

Call Sign: WB0ZQS
Karla M Dailey
1230 S Lake Dr
Watertown SD 57201

Call Sign: KF7CTI
Aric J Leadabrand
1243 S Lake Dr
Watertown SD 57201

Call Sign: KA0WOE

James F Neisen
1296 S Lake Dr
Watertown SD 57201

Call Sign: K0TY
Tony Rehder
364 S Lake Dr
Watertown SD 57201

Call Sign: N9AGG
Patricia Spieker
529 S Lake Dr
Watertown SD 57201

Call Sign: KB0NOF
Henry W German
616 S Maple
Watertown SD 572014847

Call Sign: W0MJY
James C Smith
2817 Sioux Conifer Rd
Watertown SD 57201

Call Sign: N0YZK
Eric S Tilberg
16563 Sioux Conifer Rd
Watertown SD 57201

Call Sign: KE0DX
Raymond L Russell
319 Summerwood
Watertown SD 57201

Call Sign: N0DL
David J Le Vasseur
15 Sunrise Dr
Watertown SD 572012040

Call Sign: KC0AYJ
Jan Misfatto
66 Sunrise Dr
Watertown SD 57201

Call Sign: WB0VPI

Stephen N O Brien
48 Sunrise Dr
Watertown SD 57201

Call Sign: WB0ZYR
Gene R Kluck
800 SW 10th St
Watertown SD 57201

Call Sign: W0WTN
Lake Area Radio Klub
Watertown SD 57201

Call Sign: KB0KBK
Phillip C Brugger Jr
Watertown SD 57201

Call Sign: KC0GIW
Dennis R Hetrick
Watertown SD 57201

Call Sign: N5DZX
George G Marvin
Watertown SD 572016505

FCC Amateur Radio Licenses in Waubay

Call Sign: WB0NUX
Dale L Gerriets
717 N 3rd St
Waubay SD 57273

Call Sign: W0IUK
William E Coester
3262 S Bay Dr
Waubay SD 57273

FCC Amateur Radio Licenses in Webster

Call Sign: KC0MYX
Bryan K Anderson
42766 136th St
Webster SD 57274

Call Sign: N0PTW
Paul W Dulitz
15035 438th Ave
Webster SD 57274

Call Sign: WB0SUW
Harlin G Bachmann
407 E 13th Ave
Webster SD 57274

Call Sign: KB0TYX
William D Gerriets
219 E 8th Ave
Webster SD 57274

Call Sign: W0JOZ
Lewis H Gerriets
219 E 8th Ave
Webster SD 57274

Call Sign: N0OQJ
Daniel W Dulitz
RR3
Webster SD 57274

Call Sign: WA0RGZ
Wesley Dulitz
RR3
Webster SD 572749361

Call Sign: K0FHN
Daniel P Wirtz
210 W 10th Ave
Webster SD 57274

Call Sign: WB0YPH
Merlyn R Wookey
702 W 11th Ave
Webster SD 57274

Call Sign: N0UES
Scott A Norby
514 W 5th Ave
Webster SD 57274

FCC Amateur Radio Licenses in Wecota

Call Sign: KB0NZB
Peter B Wurtz
Thunderbird Colony
Wecota SD 57438

FCC Amateur Radio Licenses in Wessington Springs

Call Sign: KB0CUJ
Thomas R Holtey
37968 221st St
Wessington Springs SD 573825215

Call Sign: KB7TFV
Mark B Major
314 5th St NE
Wessington Springs SD 57382

Call Sign: KC0CFU
James G Hurd
202 Dunham Ave N
Wessington Springs SD 573822111

Call Sign: KD0HJF
Helen L Huisman
37284 SD Hwy 34
Wessington Springs SD 57382

Call Sign: KD0HJD
Nathan R Huisman
37284 SD Hwy 34
Wessington Springs SD 57382

Call Sign: KD0AKN
Rodney G Huisman
37284 SD Hwy 34
Wessington Springs SD 57382

Call Sign: KD0HJC
Steve Vue
37284 SD Hwy 34

Wessington Springs SD 57382

Call Sign: KD0HJE
Youa Chong Vue
37284 SD Hwy 34
Wessington Springs SD 57382

Call Sign: KD0DSI
Matthew E Huisman
37284 SD Hwy 34
Wessington Springs SD 573825611

FCC Amateur Radio Licenses in Westport

Call Sign: KC5CZV
Loyd H Whatley
38648 123rd St
Westport SD 574819998

FCC Amateur Radio Licenses in White

Call Sign: WD0GVJ
Janet V Lambertus
47850 203 A St
White SD 572766030

Call Sign: KB0EF
Henry W Lambertus
47850 203 A St
White SD 572766030

Call Sign: KD0DWA
Douglas A Poss
20111 476th Ave
White SD 57276

Call Sign: N0YRU
Steven E Haase
20391 478th Ave
White SD 57276

Call Sign: W0CWW
Edmund G Schafer

20391 478th Ave
White SD 572765900

Call Sign: KD0DVX
Kristi G Lutgen
20237 485th Ave
White SD 57276

Call Sign: N0XEA
Robert H Gambill
RR2
White SD 57276

Call Sign: KC0YPX
Ingrid C Renner
White SD 57276

FCC Amateur Radio Licenses in White River

Call Sign: WB0MRK
Mark A Dewes
White River SD 57579

FCC Amateur Radio Licenses in Whitewood

Call Sign: K0EXA
John M Vainio
RR1
Whitewood SD 57793

Call Sign: N7YAO
John W Shafto
20095 Weyrich Ln
Whitewood SD 57793

Call Sign: KC0NDW
Corey L Remington
20160 Weyrich Ln
Whitewood SD 577935000

FCC Amateur Radio Licenses in Willow Lake

Call Sign: KE0DV
Gary J Neuberger
SR Box 52
Willow Lake SD 57278

Call Sign: KB0TOL
Russell H Luvaas
Willow Lake SD 57278

FCC Amateur Radio Licenses in Wilmot

Call Sign: WB0RXF
T Max Beaver
705 3rd St
Wilmot SD 57279

Call Sign: N0FSN
Maurice L Beaver
13649 465th Ave
Wilmot SD 572798010

Call Sign: W0RKZ
Charles D Floro
601 Ordway St
Wilmot SD 57279

Call Sign: N0SLA
Ardis R Mc Donald
RR1
Wilmot SD 57279

Call Sign: N0NAO
F William Whipple
RR2
Wilmot SD 57279

Call Sign: KC0DJA
Cheryl L Bassett
RR2
Wilmot SD 572799443

Call Sign: N0RXM
Daniel L Meyer
RR2

Wilmot SD 57279

Call Sign: KB0AIH
Gary L Mc Donald
13548 Valley Rd
Wilmot SD 57279

Call Sign: N0JUO
Naomi P Conrad
Wilmot SD 57279

Call Sign: N0JQE
Gerald A Doschadis
Wilmot SD 572790175

FCC Amateur Radio Licenses in Winfred

Call Sign: KA9IVJ
Richard A Galde
44253 234th St
Winfred SD 57076

Call Sign: KC0ICU
Donald A Galde II
150 Main St
Winfred SD 57076

Call Sign: N0VYS
Gerald E Gosmire
RR1
Winfred SD 57076

FCC Amateur Radio Licenses in Winner

Call Sign: K0BMQ
Richard L Faubion
433 Jefferson
Winner SD 57580

Call Sign: W0KNJ
James P Barton
842 W 10th St Apt 21
Winner SD 57580

Call Sign: WB0VJQ
Dale R Goodell
Winner SD 57580

FCC Amateur Radio Licenses in Wolsey

Call Sign: KC0KGE
Dorothy M Clouser
38936 212th St
Wolsey SD 57384

Call Sign: W0AZJ
John R Clouser
38936 212th St
Wolsey SD 57384

Call Sign: W0LWP
Henry R Bartell
20380 393 Ave
Wolsey SD 57384

Call Sign: WD0CBW
Mark D Brannen
39259 Hwy 14
Wolsey SD 57384

Call Sign: N0TDA
Robert W Taken
Wolsey SD 57384

Call Sign: KC0DKB
Gary W Quiram
Wolsey SD 573840263

FCC Amateur Radio Licenses in Wood

Call Sign: N0KMB
James M Hutchens Jr
Rt 1
Wood SD 57585

FCC Amateur Radio Licenses in Worthing

Call Sign: KB0STX
Matthew D Abbas
RR1
Worthing SD 57077

FCC Amateur Radio Licenses in Yankton

Call Sign: WA0GMH
Fred L De Roos
30971 433rd Ave
Yankton SD 57078

Call Sign: N0KXQ
Cyrus L Beye
208 Benedictine
Yankton SD 57078

Call Sign: KB0CXH
Cynthia L Nunnally
Box 15A
Yankton SD 57078

Call Sign: KB0TUG
James K Strasburg
711 Broadway
Yankton SD 57078

Call Sign: KC0BAS
Susan M Strasburg
711 Broadway
Yankton SD 57078

Call Sign: KD0YL
Myron A Schultz
2800 Broadway 51
Yankton SD 570784882

Call Sign: KB0NCK
Tomas G Olson
Brodway
Yankton SD 57078

Call Sign: WB0WCT
Robert W Hanson
813 Burgess Rd
Yankton SD 57078

Call Sign: W8MHW
Bruce H Brazelton
2508 Capitol St
Yankton SD 57078

Call Sign: KC0MOI
Richard V Wilkerson
1213 Cedar St
Yankton SD 57078

Call Sign: KT3J
Frank W Heemstra
900 E 18th St
Yankton SD 570782413

Call Sign: KB0RG
Frank E Hoxsie
208 E 31st St
Yankton SD 57078

Call Sign: N0MHL
Marvin L Olnes Jr
1204 Green St
Yankton SD 57078

Call Sign: KC0CXR
Claris R Kelly
1401 Green St
Yankton SD 57078

Call Sign: W0WZA
Timothy J Kelly
1401 Green St
Yankton SD 57078

Call Sign: N0BZP
James W Farley
1005 Kennedy Dr
Yankton SD 57078

Call Sign: WB0NEH
Marvin L Miller
131 Kniest Ave
Yankton SD 570786741

Call Sign: NU0D
Terry J Gorham
Linn St
Yankton SD 570784215

Call Sign: NU0E
Terry J Gorham
Linn St
Yankton SD 570784215

Call Sign: KB0PGZ
Robert R Schultz
1700 Locust Apt 313
Yankton SD 57078

Call Sign: N0QJL
George Kamenar
313 Maple
Yankton SD 57078

Call Sign: KB0NCJ
Kenneth P Peterka
1202 Maple St
Yankton SD 57078

Call Sign: KB0MFO
Daniel L Gran
2105 Mulberry
Yankton SD 57078

Call Sign: K0WIU
William N Jennewein
302 Northern Ave
Yankton SD 57078

Call Sign: N0UPE
Douglas M Jennewein
302 Northern Ave
Yankton SD 57078

Call Sign: WB0FMD
Shirley M Jennewein
302 Northern Ave
Yankton SD 57078

Call Sign: KE0FQ
George F Smith
1603 Picotte
Yankton SD 57078

Call Sign: N0DDU
Delmer L Vennard
609 Picotte St
Yankton SD 570784129

Call Sign: KC4JRO
Stephen L Gregory
RR1
Yankton SD 57078

Call Sign: KB0CXI
Dennis M Nunnally
RR1
Yankton SD 57078

Call Sign: KB0MLC
Owen J Cowles
RR1
Yankton SD 57078

Call Sign: KB0MLD
Jason G Cwach
RR2
Yankton SD 57078

Call Sign: NX0F
Chris L Nelson
RR2
Yankton SD 57078

Call Sign: KC4JSB
Patti A Gregory
Rt 1
Yankton SD 57078

Call Sign: KA0IFL
William H Bergman
43384 SD Hwy 52
Yankton SD 57078

Call Sign: N0PJ
Paul J Aughenbaugh
109 Sherwood Dr
Yankton SD 570786715

Call Sign: W0YSD
Scott D Anderson
415 Spruce St
Yankton SD 57078

Call Sign: KN0GOD
Dee Rhonda L Anderson
415 Spruce St
Yankton SD 57078

Call Sign: KB0RUE
Scott D Anderson
415 Spruce St
Yankton SD 57078

Call Sign: KB0RWE
Dee Rhonda L Anderson
415 Spruce St
Yankton SD 57078

Call Sign: KC0CXQ
Timothy J Kelly
417 Spruce St
Yankton SD 570783827

Call Sign: KC0MOH
Michael D Daniels
1401 Sunrise Dr
Yankton SD 57078

Call Sign: W0MDD
Michael D Daniels
1401 Sunrise Dr
Yankton SD 57078

Call Sign: KD0ACR
Richard J Schwartzmyer
119 Tamarack St
Yankton SD 57078

Call Sign: W2RZM
William H Lippert
1004 W 10th St
Yankton SD 57078

Call Sign: AA0RM
Hans Schwarz
908 W 11th St
Yankton SD 57078

Call Sign: KB0EZW
Jerold D Sorbel
903 W 15 St
Yankton SD 57078

Call Sign: WB0VEU
Leona M Cowles
203 W 25th St
Yankton SD 570781319

Call Sign: WB0VEV
James L Cowles
203 W 25th St
Yankton SD 570781319

Call Sign: N0JPL
Kenneth L Buhl
204 Walnut
Yankton SD 57078

Call Sign: KC0KZM
Linda D Gorham
1204 Whiting St
Yankton SD 57078

Call Sign: N0IGP
Terry J Gorham
1204 Whiting St
Yankton SD 570782507

Call Sign: KC0LOE
Daniel R Fields
1404 Whiting St
Yankton SD 57078

Call Sign: K0YG
Daniel R Fields
1404 Whiting St
Yankton SD 57078

Call Sign: KB0MFR
John S Lorenz
Yankton SD 57078

Call Sign: N0TCV
Mary K Adam
Yankton SD 57078

Call Sign: AE0P
Brian D Adam
Yankton SD 57078

www.ingramcontent.com/pod-product-compliance
Lightning Source LLC
Chambersburg PA
CBHW082132290526

45794CB00008B/3009